To Judy —

Thank you for your support & all you do. Best always,

Pat Givin

THE BERKELEY MARINA MURDERS:

ONE FAMILY'S STORY

PATRICIA M. GIOIA

ISBN 0-7414-3539-X

Published by:

INFI∞ITY
PUBLISHING.COM

1094 New DeHaven Street, Suite 100
West Conshohocken, PA 19428-2713
Info@buybooksontheweb.com
www.buybooksontheweb.com
Toll-free (877) BUY BOOK
Local Phone (610) 941-9999
Fax (610) 941-9959

Printed in the United States of America

Printed on Recycled Paper

Published September 2006

For my daughter, Mary Regina,
and her friend, Gregory Allen Kniffin
and for
Joan
Christine
Gerard
Lawrence
Robert
Patrick
and
Daniel

TABLE OF CONTENTS

Appendix

ACKNOWLEDGMENTS

Writing Mary's story might be compared to a bud on a rose bush waiting to bloom. Its content was deeply implanted in my mind but needed time to blossom forth. Also needed were the "gardeners" who did the weeding and feeding – in the form of suggesting and prodding – who said, "Write it!" Thanks to all of them, I finally did.

I will attempt to acknowledge the many people who helped as I struggled to put this into words. If I overlook anyone, it is not done intentionally. There were just so many of you.

Of course, my family was always there, supportive and loving, allowing Mom to tell our story. I thank each one especially for sharing their painful recollections of the aftermath of their sister's death. An added note of appreciation goes to Joan for sharing her journal writings; her words helped to fill out the story.

Posthumously, I thank my faithful friend, Jean Stirpe, to whom I owe so much. The generosity she showed my family when we were out in California at the trials was truly extraordinary. I cannot imagine what our experience would have been without Jean always being there, offering us bed, board and her loving friendship. Sadly, Jean died in January 2005. So many times, as I wrote this story, I wanted to pick up the phone and check out a fact with her. I regret that I could not do that.

David Kniffin, Greg's dad, and Dorothy, David's sister, stood side by side with my family and me as we struggled with the pain of Mary and Greg's murders. I appreciated their generosity and friendship, and the loan of the VW Bug during the trials was a lifesaver for us.

In depicting a more intimate picture of Mary, I incorporated writings and thoughts from family members and some of her close friends. I am grateful to all of them for their insights.

I thank Carrie Freitag, a member of POMC, and the sister of William Herbert Freitag, a victim of homicide in 1998, for graciously allowing me to quote from her insightful book, <u>Aftermath, In the Wake of Murder</u>. And my gratitude to Mary Elledge, mother of Rob, murdered in 1986, for granting permission to include her beautiful poem, "The Fallen Flower," which almost appeared to be written for our family too.

The encouragement and support of my friends in the Niskayuna Writing Group, who said this story had to be written, were major motivators in my getting it done! In particular, Janet Evans became my hero as she edited and re-edited my manuscript, always professionally, gracefully and with love. I could not have done it without her guidance and support. I'm grateful too to my longtime friend, Doris Aiken, who prodded me many times when I felt I could not write this, but Doris insisted I could.

A story like ours, involving the criminal justice system, has other important players who need to be acknowledged and thanked. Chief among them are Assistant District Attorney Jim Anderson, who fought long and hard to achieve justice for Mary and Greg, and won the successful conviction of their murderer. I am grateful to Fred Eihl and Dan Wolke, the two detectives, who were resolute in their pursuit of Mary's and Greg's killer and showed compassion and friendship to my family and me.

After conviction and sentencing, our case moved on to the California Attorney General's Office. Assistant

Attorney Generals Gerald A. Engler (Jerry) and Dane R. Gillette have continued to be supportive of our lingering concerns, and carry on the fight for justice for Mary and Greg.

The list of those who helped me in its writing could probably go on and on, but then you mightn't have time to read Mary's story.

The Fallen Flower

While looking at our poster,
We hope you can see
How much our bouquet
Is like a family.
A radiant rose has fallen
Like a life;
But why we ask,
Must there be so much strife.
Tears fall
When a loved one is gone;
They form a pool that goes on and on.
Like the poster,
The bouquet still
Remains intact;
We all know our loved
One won't be back.
So help us see the beauty
In our fallen flower;
We'll try not to let the grief
Overpower.
Now you can see
How much the bouquet is like a family.

Written by Mary Elledge, Greater Portland POMC Chapter

PREFACE

The rose is ***the*** *most prominent image in the human brain, as to delicacy, beauty, short-livedness, thorniness... There is no better allegory for, dare I say it, life, than roses.* Robert Hunter, <u>Grateful Dead – the music never stopped.</u>

Our family's symbol for Mary is the rose. It represents her beauty, her delicate nature, her short life. Its thorns equate her horrible death and our terrible feeling of loss.

We continue to think of Mary as our rose. This beautiful flower, beloved by so many, was her hallmark. She filled her sketchbook with roses, and when she signed her name, Mary, it often spiraled, ending as a tiny rosebud. On a Valentine's Day card Mary once sent, with a radiant red rose pictured on the front, was the sentiment written by Hadin Marshall, "The rose speaks of love silently, in a language known only to the heart."

After Mary's death, I collected countless newspaper articles, made endless notes of telephone conversations, and filled box upon box with legal documents, all relating to our court case. It is an inventory of pain, with nothing discarded, because I promised Mary one day I would tell her story.

It's been more than twenty years since our rose was snatched from our family. I find I am in a different place than when it happened. But it's an important, albeit painful, part of our family history. We were all changed by her murder. I will attempt to tell the story of how we survived the worst experience a family can go through, and how we continue to cope with the loss of a beloved daughter and sister. I will tell it as best I can and as I remember it.

Our rose now grows in another garden, sorely missed, but her spirit continues strong with all her family. I know Mary was with me as I wrote her story.

1

FRIDAY

Friday, August 16, 1985 - Heading home after a week's camping at Fish Creek Pond in the Adirondacks, Moises is at the wheel of his prized dark gray Chevrolet truck. I sit next to him and am anxious to get home. With our marriage struggling, the three-hour drive back to Schenectady afforded us more time to talk things over. It's the second marriage for each of us and it's proving to be a difficult mix. I knew it would be a monumental task to incorporate Moises into a family of eight children but since most were now out of the house, living on their own, I thought it would work. At least I remained somewhat optimistic.

About 6 p.m, we pulled into the driveway. Dan, my youngest, greeted us briefly, "How was the camping, Mom? The weather, good?"

"It was great. Hot, but not too much and we had a fairly good campsite."

Dan was back from college for the summer and had a job with the Town Highway Department. He soon left with friends for a Friday night out. Immediately Moises began unpacking our month's worth of luggage. Gone for only a week, he made sure we were not caught unprepared! Before I began to help, and trying to avert any further problems, I dashed into the house to check things out. I quickly assessed the first floor rooms for any evidence of partying that might have taken place while we were away. Other than discarding a few empty plastic cups from on top of the refrigerator, the house appeared neat. Dan did well.

A pile of mail sat on the dining room table. I was excited

to see an envelope addressed to me. It read *Mama Gioia-Riano* and was postmarked August 13, Oakland, California. In the corner, in multicolored letters was written *Long Lost D., Mary, Santa Cruz, CA*. My heart leapt - a letter from Mary. Since she left for California about six weeks ago, we spoke only once. I recalled the date, July 13th, the day of the first Live-AID concert. In the middle of painting the side door stairwell and listening to the concert on the radio, the phone rang. I answered.

"Hi, Ma, it's me, Mary. Just thought I'd give you a call while I can. How's everything at home?'

Thrilled to hear her voice, I said, "Let me put my paint brush down. It's so good to talk to you. Joan told me you've been in touch with her a few times about your cat, Samson. How do you like California?"

"Mom, it's great. It's very different from home. You wouldn't believe these mountains out here. They're so beautiful. And things are going good - am traveling up and down the state looking for somewhere to live and to find a job."

We chatted for a few more minutes. She promised that when she had a mailing address for me, she'd call.

With these thoughts running through my mind, I set the envelope aside, like a delicious dessert, to return to later. Now I had better help Moises unpack our camping gear.

When I finished, I climbed the stairs to the second floor bedroom. I made myself comfortable on the bed and picked up my precious letter. Now, at last I could read it.

As I opened the envelope, I smiled. There were seven pages in all, yellow, pink, orange, blue and white, a rainbow of colors. Her stationery was directed towards me, the occasional activist, as she wrote on the backs of local "protest sheets." She knew I would relish her choice of writing paper.

The first page, a bright yellow, shouted out an appeal to join the Coalition to Stop Food Irradiation. Mary scribbled, "Read this and weep! We must stop this terrible process." She intended to send a copy to the co-op she frequented in Albany. Next, a deep pink colored sheet announced "Down on the Factory Farm," a film produced by an Animal Rights Action Group. Page 3 was a flyer for "Update Nicaragua," a community public affairs radio show, and page 6, a small blue handbill, advertised a Santa Cruz production of Gore Vidal's comedy, "Visit

14

to a Small Planet." I pictured her smiling as she wrote on the top of the last page, "Oh no, another piece of paper." This one publicized a Nuclear War Crimes Tribunal in Berkeley to remember the 40th anniversary of Hiroshima/Nagasaki.

When I finished reading all of the pages, out fell a comical newspaper article about "Chumley the cat," which read, "Sgt. Chumley has been booted out of the Police Department." Apparently, Chumley contracted fleas and could no longer be of service. Mary thought it would be great for our refrigerator and that "Moises will be lovin it!" Wise to the uneasy home situation, she wrote she trusted Gato (our cat) and Moises were doing fine and getting along and hoped her brother, Lieny (Dan) was getting in shape for football.

She said she was writing the letter while in a coffee shop in Santa Cruz, "sippin some coffee!" Mary enjoyed a nonchalant manner of writing, eliminating last letters on words. She said her lengthy letter was to save me another collect call from California.

Her letter described some jobs she was looking into. One at a ski resort at Lake Tahoe, or "northern California...where it's at for me these days! Up in the mountains, it's so beautiful."

She thought I might be "freaked out about these plans." She and a friend were plotting to go to Guatemala in January for a month to learn weaving.

> We'll either rent a car or take a train through Mexico to Guatemala .We can either stay in hotels for cheap or live w/a family! And we would both rather live w/a family! Weaving is something I've always had a desire to learn!
>
> I may have a possibility of working in a nice expensive restaurant in Oakland—not sure yet, have to talk to my friend. So anyways! I know I won't like Oakland! But if I can make a lot of $ to save I'll do it!

I laughed as she described a "pretty neat job in San Francisco—a bike messenger!" But she thought this might be a bit dangerous.

She ended with,

> *At my friend Rusty's near the ocean in Santa Cruz, not too far anyway. If I listen for it I hear the waves crashing in....Remember I love you! and everyone else too! See you or probably call you soon!*
> > *Your long lost - ever lovin, daughter,*
> > *Mary Regina.*

I hadn't realized, I suppose, that she often used both names, Mary and Regina. She really liked her two names. Most of us called her Mary or shortened, "Mare." Her brothers and their friends, with playful teen-age humor, said first names backwards so she was dubbed "Yram."

The telephone on the nightstand rang just as I finished reading the letter. I answered. The person at the other end identified herself as from the Niskayuna Police. She wanted to make sure I was at home. "Is there anyone else there with you?" she inquired. I told her yes; my husband was home too. I thought those strange questions, but I replied to both in the affirmative.

A few minutes later the doorbell rang. I carefully put the letter aside and went downstairs to open the front door. Two solemn-looking policemen stood in the doorway

"Mrs. Gioia? May we come in? Is your husband here?"

Nervously, I replied, "Yes, please come in."

As I led them into the living room, my mind raced to Dan. Had something happened to him, still out with friends?

They asked Moises and me to sit down, making sure we were both comfortably seated.

Their first question took me off guard, "Do you have a daughter, Mary?"

I replied, nervously, "Yes."

"Is she in California?"

I responded quickly, "Yes, I was just upstairs reading a letter from her."

Their next words remain forever imbedded in my mind, "We're sorry. She's dead."

I screamed, "NO, NO, IT CAN'T BE! I WAS JUST READING HER LETTER!"

16

"She was found in San Francisco Bay."

Somehow I gathered enough strength to utter, "But she was a good swimmer. Are you saying she drowned?"

"No, she was shot."

"OH, MY GOD", I screamed and wailed. MY MARY SHOT! MY MARY DEAD!

The officers told us that the Berkeley Police contacted the Niskayuna Police earlier that night. I don't remember saying anything more, perhaps a whispered thank you. They gave us a phone number for the police in Berkeley but since it was almost midnight we would have to wait until morning to get more information from California. So I was left with the horror of knowing so little about Mary's death, except that she was dead.

Moises attempted to calm me. He too was very upset. Despite all their problems, he did love Mary. But at that moment he didn't know how to comfort me. Who would? He talked about Mary having gone to California. His next words probably helped to seal his fate with me.

"Pat, I told you so. You shouldn't have let her go out there."

Somehow I managed to answer, "It wasn't my decision. Mary was 22, and she's been on her own for the last few years. It was her dream to go out west. I don't think I could have stopped her."

.

2

LATER THAT NIGHT

Still reeling from the horrific news of Mary's death, I knew I needed to notify the rest of the family. It's the hardest thing I ever did - to tell her brothers and sisters that she was dead—murdered. I telephoned Joan, the oldest and the only one living nearby. She wasn't home. Joan was a nurse at St. Clare's Hospital; her husband, Mike, told me she was still at work.

I sputtered out, incoherently, "Mike, something terrible happened to Mary. She was shot. She's dead. I need to reach Joan."

Mike called Joan at work. When she came to the phone, he told her something had happened. She needed to come home right away.

Recognizing the anxiety in his voice, she screamed into the phone, "What happened?"

Mike blurted out, "It's Mary. She's dead."

Joan screamed, "No! Oh, God, no! I'll go to Mom's right away." She asked a co-worker for a ride; she knew she couldn't drive. Dashing into the house, she ran to me, still in her white uniform, her eyes red from hot tears. She screamed for answers I did not have.

"What happened? Oh, Mom, no, no, not Mary! Please tell me it's not so."

I hugged my eldest as if she too would disappear if I let her go. Nine years separated them but Joan and Mary were very close. As Mary grew into a teenager, they vacationed together several times, and when Joan's daughter, Amanda, was born,

Mary was the only babysitter Joan entrusted her with the first month. Mary lived with Joan for several months before going to California. Joan was the last family member to see her before she left. Now, Joan, Moises and I stood in the kitchen, talking, crying, not knowing what to do next.

At that moment, we heard Gerard (Gerry), my eldest son, drive into the backyard. Gerry, a school psychologist in Maryland, and Margie, his wife of a few months, planned to spend a week at home. One of Gerry's friends was to be married, and Gerry was invited to the wedding. Joan quickly ran out on the porch to reach him before he came in. Gerry looked surprised to see Joan standing there on the back porch, still in her uniform.

As she ran to him, she whimpered, "Mary's dead—murdered."

When Gerry heard this, he broke down, crying as if his heart was breaking. Gerry was very much like his father, Vito, even down to his chosen profession, both psychologists. Gerry had a strong sense of duty to me and the rest of the family. Often an advisor on family problems, I'm sure at that moment he searched his mind for what he could have done to prevent this.

Gerry ran into the kitchen, practically knocking me over, pleading, "What happened, Mom? Is it true?"

Shaking still, I moaned, "Yes, honey. I'm afraid so."

I repeated what the Niskayuna Police told me only an hour before and that we had to wait until morning to get more complete details. We cried; we hugged one another; we avoided the difficult task at hand—notifying the others. Finally, Joan, exhibiting remarkable strength, picked up the phone to call her brother, Lawrence.

The family calls him Lawr. To everyone else, he is known as Larry. He and his wife, Mary Ann, lived in Hartsdale, near White Plains. Lawr was working on an M.B.A. at Columbia University School of Business. He had been a great help to me after his father was gone. Lawr graduated with a degree in marine engineering and worked for Exxon Oil Company for several years. His two months' on, two months' off schedule allowed him time to help me at home with his younger siblings. Now it was so hard to tell him about Mary. When she bought her first—and only—car, Lawr went with her to "check it out." Yes, he said, the 1977 Plymouth Volare would be okay.

19

When Lawr heard the news of Mary's death, he broke down. Sobbing, he said to Joan, "I'll come right home. Now, tonight."

We knew he would be in no condition to drive the three hours up the winding Taconic Parkway, so we persuaded him not to come that night. Fortunately, Mary Ann, an optometrist, had to work the next day, Saturday, so they decided they would drive up together after she finished.

Years later, Lawr told me that next day was one of the worst days of his life. Images of Mary, unsophisticated, guileless, loving, most of all, happy, kept jumping before him. He couldn't bear hanging around the apartment all day by himself. He walked the streets, searching out a local music store. There he found Bob Dylan's haunting piece, "Forever Young." He tucked the music and words into his mind. It would be used later at Mary's burial. Lawr knew this about Mary - she would be forever young.

We paced around the kitchen and dining room - what to do next? We needed to contact Mary's three siblings living in Boston. Of those, Christine and her husband, Jeff, were the first to move "east." Robert and Patrick followed in that order after graduating from college. Boston was a haven for jobs and exciting city life.

Joan attempted to telephone Christine. Standing there, I thought, how do you tell someone that her birthday sister is dead? Mary and Christine were both born on December 20th, eight years apart. The telephone rang and rang. No answer. Then Joan proceeded to call Robert. She amazed me as she shored up enough strength to finish this dreadful task. Joan said she doesn't remember crying much that night. She was too numb and in shock, as we all were.

Rob lived in Malden, a little north of Boston. He and his future wife, Brenda, had an apartment there. After finishing college at the Rochester Institute of Technology (RIT), with a degree in business administration, Rob moved to Boston and worked in sales there for several years. The phone was next to the bed. When it rang, Brenda answered.

Joan said, "Can I talk to Rob?"

Brenda recognized that something was wrong when Joan asked to speak to Rob, not chatting at all with her. She handed Rob the phone.

"Rob, it's Joan. I have bad news. It's Mary. She's dead."

Robert said he remembers falling back on the bed, unable to move, unable to speak. Joan told him the little we knew. When Rob collected himself, he told Joan he would go over to Patrick's and to Christine's. He wanted to tell them the terrible news in person. Rob and Brenda were packing, preparing to leave early the next morning with friends for a camping trip up in Maine. If Joan had not reached him then, it would have been very difficult to locate them after they left on their trip. Now, Rob and Brenda immediately drove over to Patrick's apartment in West Roxbury.

Rob, Patrick, Mary and Dan shared a special place in our family. As the four youngest, they were dubbed "the little grubs," a term dreamed up by their two older brothers. They shared many mutual experiences together, one being devotees of the Grateful Dead. Perhaps this made their bond even tighter.

Rob and Brenda arrived at Patrick's. He had been out that night at a party at his friend, Brad Roberts'. In the early to mid-80s, Boston was a haven for many of their Niskayuna friends. They found jobs and each other there. At one time, they tried to persuade Mary to come and work in Boston too after graduating from Schenectady County Community College. But she was more of a "country girl," choosing to work at Lake George and Vermont.

Patrick arrived home late that night from Brad's. Having just gone to bed, he heard a noise that sounded like rocks hitting his window. Half asleep, he peered out and saw Robert and Brenda. His doorbell didn't work; they had to arouse him some way. Patrick, surprised to see them, wondered why they had come all the way over to his apartment at that late hour.

Letting them in, Patrick said, "Whoa! What brings you both over here? Is something wrong?"

Somehow, Rob managed to say, "It's Mary. Something has happened and she's dead."

Patrick later told me, "At that moment, my knees gave way; I fell on the floor; everything inside me collapsed." When Rob said she was shot, his first thoughts were maybe she was in a drug deal gone badly. But then thought *Oh, no, not our sweet Mary.*

The two brothers remained locked to one another, not wanting to let go. Then Patrick said, "I need to talk to Mom."

When I heard Patrick's voice on the other end of the line,

it was hard to speak.

He mumbled, "Mom, I can't believe it! Mary, dead! I don't know how I'm going to go on. How do you do it? I know you've dealt with Grandma's death and Grandpa's. But, Mary!"

I realized he was hurting so much by the news. I managed to say, "I know, Patrick. Somehow, some way, we'll get through this together. Now, it's important for you to take care of yourself. Please drive safely and I'll see you tomorrow. I love you. Now, let me talk to Rob again."

Rob and I spoke for another few minutes. He said he and Brenda and Pat would drive over to Jamaica Plain to tell Chris, whom we were still not able to reach by phone. She, the birthday sister, would be almost the last to know.

Christine arrived home after an evening out with a girlfriend. The telephone rang as she went in the door. She thought it must be Jeff, her husband. He was back home in Amsterdam, New York, for a family celebration for his mother. Chris wasn't able to go with him as she had to work. She was a diet technician at the New England Deaconess Hospital. Now she grabbed the phone.

She heard Joan at the other end, crying and saying, "Chris, Mary's dead."

Christine reeled backwards, trying to make some sense out of what she thought she heard.

"What did you say? Oh, no!"

At that very moment, Rob, Patrick and Brenda appeared at her door. Red-eyed and visibly shaking, they all had the same message: Mary had been shot in California. She was dead. The four stayed together for another hour, hugging, crying, and making plans to go back to Schenectady.

At home, we still had to tell Dan, who had gone out with friends for the night. Dan was the youngest, next to Mary. We worried he might hear the awful news on the radio or television before we could tell him. We weren't sure if the local media had picked up on the story. Joan pinpointed a few places where her brother might have gone. Then, she, Gerry and Margie set out on their mournful mission.

Dan was at a nightclub, now known as "Saratoga Winners." Slipknot, a local band that played Grateful Dead music, was performing there. When the trio arrived, they ran into some of Dan's friends but he wasn't with them. They paged Dan. When he heard his name over the loudspeaker, he ran over to them. He was dumbfounded to see Joan, still in her uniform, with Gerry and Margie standing there too. Surmising something must be dreadfully wrong, he gathered enough courage to say, "What's up? What are you guys doing here?"

Joan hugged him and quietly said, "Mary's been murdered."

Shocked, hardly able to speak, Dan left immediately with Joan, Gerry and Margie. Driving back to the house, not much was said among the four. Not much was known. Just lots of sobbing and desperate cries of "Why? Why?"

When they arrived home, Dan raced to me in the kitchen. Angry, confused, he sobbed over and over, "She used to hit me over the head with the telephone. She used to hit me over the head with the telephone." A mantra as he tried to deal with his grief.

Now everyone had been told. Joan, Gerry, Margie, Dan, and I sat around for a while, talking, huddling, crying. The last few hours had been filled with unspeakable pain. Moises had already gone to bed.

Dan and I drove Joan home to her husband, Mike, and their little girl, Amanda, then 18 months old. Amanda would be my only grandchild who knew her Aunt Mary.

Joan later wrote in her journal, "When I got home that night, I couldn't sleep. I collected all of the things Mary had stored in the kitchen and bathroom when she lived with us. I put them together in a box." She's not sure why she did that. Perhaps it was an act of finality. Mary would not be back to use them.

Somehow we all made it through to the next morning. I don't think I slept for three, four, maybe more nights. Mary appeared before me but I could not reach her.

3

SATURDAY

August 17th – Thus began our second day of agony. Heading down to the kitchen, I walked as if my feet were not attached to my body, my mind muddled. Was this all a nightmare or had the police really been here last night? When I saw Gerry sitting there, his head in his hands, and Joan, looking pale and worn, I knew it was real.

Moises came downstairs, joining us. Looking over at Gerry, he began, "Your mother was talking in her sleep all night. I couldn't quiet her."

I overheard him but wasn't sure if his concern was for me or for his own lack of sleep. I remained cool towards him. Last night, his remarks about allowing Mary to go out to California deeply disturbed me. Was I really to blame? Could I have stopped her? Over the years, I searched for what I could have done differently, for this not to happen. There has never been an answer.

Joan said, "I couldn't sleep at all, Mom. I drove over to the hospital early this morning to get my makeup kit, which I left there in my rush to get here last night."

While at St. Clare's, she talked for a while with one of her co-workers, the first non-family member she could pour her heart out to. Then arriving at the house, she saw Gerry and Dan. She hugged them both and asked Dan, "Did you sleep?"

"Not much. I still can't believe it."

Dan would have a very hard time accepting his sister's

24

death. Dan and Mary were the two youngest, the last to live at home. They had their share of harmless family feuds when young. Dan could be annoying to his sister and vice versa. A note they wrote me years before, and which I kept, illustrated this.

> Mom —
> *We are sorry we made you mad. But little brothers can be pains sometimes and so can big sisters. We hope you aren't too mad at us.*
> *Love, (s) Mary (s) Dan* (after which he wrote, *Excellent signature*)
> *P.S. Sorry we aren't up to say it but I went to bed early so I could get up early. And so did Leinad.*
> *P.S.S. Can you put my wash in the dryer for me. Please?*
> *Thanks*

When I read this, I always smile. First, there's the plea for forgiveness, followed by a request for help.

Joan left after a short time spent talking with her brothers. On the way home, she stopped at St. Helen's, the nearby church where we had been parishioners for many years. Finding the church door locked, her car became her chapel, praying as she drove the few blocks to her house. She was exhausted when she arrived. She tried to sleep. After tossing and turning for about an hour, she came back to the house. She needed to be with the rest of the family. Little Amanda stayed with Joan's in-laws for several days while everything was in such a turmoil.

The local media were already stirring. CNN had a clip of Mary being dragged out of the water. We hadn't seen it yet but I could only imagine how ghastly it would be when we did, realizing this was our Mary. We also needed to know how to respond to questions that would surely soon be asked.

At noon we called California. The time differential and the 3,000 miles between New York and California were hurdles to overcome, especially in the early days of our case. I asked Gerry to make the call to the Berkeley police. He would ask questions I could not ask. Gerry was an amazing source of strength

25

for me in those first days. He spoke to the Homicide Division of the Berkeley Police Department and to the Alameda County Coroner's Office. How hard it must have been for him as he heard a candid description of what had happened to his sister.

Gerry learned that Mary was found in the waters of San Francisco Bay near a rocky shore, south of a place called Rainbow Village. Then he heard the gory details of how she died. There was a gunshot entrance in the right side of her neck, possibly done by a 30-caliber rifle. Her body had been taken to a hospital. Gerry was told a formal report would be issued in three to four weeks. Mary was identified by her driver's license and also by a young man, Robin Van Heest, who had been with her shortly before her death. The coroner's office told Gerry that we should proceed with funeral arrangements here and to have our funeral director contact them.

The cruel invasion of privacy murder victims endure, their bodies pored over and examined by complete strangers. When I pictured Mary undergoing such treatment, I was deeply pained. No one from her family with her. I knew it was her physical body that was examined and probed, her spirit had long since gone. But this was the body that grew in mine for nine months! She would always be my baby, my little girl.

Gerry wrote down snippets of his conversation with the Berkeley Police. We learned more gruesome details of what happened. Both Inspector Dan Wolke and Detective Fred Eihl had been at the scene and reported this:

"At 11:15am on Friday, August 16th, we (Berkeley Police) received a call from a man who had been walking his dog by the marina. He spotted something or someone floating face down in the water, about 15 feet from shore."

Since Mary had been shot by a high-powered rifle, they concluded it was definitely a murder. Inspector Wolke told Gerry something unusual took place as Mary was brought to shore. A crowd of people from Rainbow Village had assembled at the water's edge to see what all the excitement was about. One man muttered, "That looks like Mary."

Inspector Wolke turned around to see who said this because at the time it was difficult to tell what was being dragged in from the water, no less to be able to identify it as male or female. He asked David Elliott, a fellow officer at the scene, if he knew who the man was who had spoken. Elliott told him he was "International." Wolke had a faint recognition of that name but didn't recognize the other name the man used, Ralph Thomas. Later, when Wolke returned to the police station, he ran it through the computer system and discovered the long history of felonies International or Ralph Thomas had on his record.

Wolke continued telling Gerry, "We have a dive team at this very moment searching the waters for the gun and possibly another body. When we questioned a young man, Robin van Heest, he identified the body as Mary. She had been with him at a party outside a van on Thursday night and left the party with a young man named Greg. They had all been drinking and smoking pot." After the police spoke to him, Robin was allowed to leave town as he appeared to be non-violent and not involved in the murder.

Wolke surmised Mary and Greg came back to the area around 3am. Either Greg had killed Mary and left the Village or he too was dead. But people they spoke to were convinced Greg would not have killed Mary.

Mary's wallet and driver's license were found. It was speculated that she had been at Rainbow Village for two nights. Gerry, not knowing anything about Rainbow Village, asked Wolke about it. Wolke gave a brief description. The City of Berkeley opened it in January 1985 as an experiment in response to complaints about people living out of cars, crowding city streets. They designated an area across from the city at the Berkeley landfill where people could live out of their vehicles for a small rental fee. At this time, there was a community of about 20 cars there, with both homeless and older hippie types. Followers of the Grateful Dead band also congregated between shows in two buses parked at the Village. This was probably why Mary was there.

While Gerry spoke to the police, Greg was found. In the margin of his notes, Gerry wrote, "Just found 2nd body in bay." We learned Greg had been buried in the same murky waters and that he too had been shot with a high-powered rifle. Immediately, we thought, "OH GOD, ANOTHER GRIEVING FAMILY!"

The police gave Gerry a few more details. They thought Mary was murdered about 75 yards from the road leading into Rainbow Village. Blood had been discovered near a tractor there. But the area had already been paved over because the site was a landfill. Precious evidence may have been lost. Crime scenes are generally secured until an investigation is completed. Usually only a short space of time exists when evidence can be collected. In our case, whoever paved over the area certainly was not in the loop of the investigation.

Gerry asked the police, "Why do you think Mary was killed? Do you have an idea of the motive?"

Since International's prior felony history was on record, they surmised it was probably a sexual assault, gone bad.

Then Wolke warned Gerry: "Don't reveal any of what we have told you to the local media. We're still investigating and we may have a suspect. If it gets out, he might run."

"Okay, what can we say to the media?"

"Just talk about Mary, who she was and what she was doing out here in California."

Even though, by now, we were relatively certain it was our Mary who had been found, Inspector Wolke asked that we send her dental records to complete the identification. We telephoned our good friend and family dentist, John Principe. After telling him what happened to Mary, we asked that he send her records to California by overnight mail. Unfortunately, they bore out our worst fears. It was Mary.

4

SATURDAY AFTERNOON

During the afternoon the rest of the family trickled home to 4 Cornelius Avenue. Two houses in off Union Street in the Town of Niskayuna, Schenectady County, we called this home since 1957. Five of our eight children joined our family while we lived there. Dubbed a Dutch Colonial by our realtor, the house was built in the early 1900s and stretched three stories upward at its highest peak. In the late 1970s, a more attractive Wedgewood Blue aluminum siding replaced its original drab gray asphalt siding.

Christine and Patrick drove in together from Boston. Patrick sat quietly in the passenger seat. More recently he recalled, "I don't know how Chris did it. She drove through a storm of tears." An hour later Rob and Brenda, along with their dog, Jessie, jumping in the back seat, pulled in. Lastly, Chris' husband, Jeffrey, drove over from Amsterdam, bringing along their dog, Chee. For several days, Joan's small bungalow on Dean Street became a bulging boarding house for three couples, a two-year old, and two dogs. Lawrence and Mary Ann arrived last. Our family was now complete, minus one.

As each arrived, we hugged, we cried, we tried to console one another. We wandered into the dining room and sat around the large mahogany table where so many joyful events took place. It was where we came together for family meals each night. It was where we held holiday, birthday, graduation, and even wedding celebrations. It was where family discussions were held and decisions made, some serious, some trivial. Now we sat together in that same room, at that same table, making decisions, like none we ever had before. Unanswered questions about what happened to Mary continued to plague us. Who did this horrendous deed, murdering two young, innocent people? Why? We read about murders in the daily newspaper, see the grieving families on evening television, but you never believe it will happen in your family—to your loved one.

We talked about what we had to do next. Uppermost in our minds was whether I, or someone in the family, should go out to California to view the body, to make certain it was really our Mary. Joan came up with an excellent suggestion. "Why don't we call Uncle Joe, Mom? Maybe he could help us decide."

Joseph Gioia, my late husband Vito's older brother, was a pathologist and at that time Chief Medical Officer at St. Francis Hospital in Poughkeepsie. He and his wife, Tina, were always close to our children.

"Good idea," I said, picking up the phone. Joe was shocked, saddened and angry when he heard the reason for my call. I told him as much as the police informed us.

"The police are reasonably certain it's Mary. A young man who had been with her that day identified her. They also found her wallet and driver's license. What do you think? Should I go out to be sure? We're really struggling with the decision and that's why I thought if we spoke to you, you might advise us what's best."

Joe spoke calmly, saying, "Pat, I don't think it's necessary for one of you to go to California. From what you've told me, it sounds like everything possible to identify Mary has been done."

I told him we would discuss it further but was relieved to hear it might not be necessary for us to make the long trip out there.

Joe said, "Pat, I'm so very sorry. I wish one of us could be up there to help. Let us know if there's anything we can do."

When I hung up the phone, our discussion continued but armed with Joe's comments, we decided to have Mary returned to us, without going out to identify her. We then spoke about cremation. From all we had learned about the state of her body, that seemed best solution. It would not be the first time someone in the family was cremated. After his death in 1977, Vito had been cremated.

Gerry, with tears in his eyes, looked at me, saying, "Mom, I think that's what Mary would want."

Everyone agreed but Joan uttered what was in all of our minds, "This means we'll never see Mary again. Oh, God, if only I could have something of Mary's to make it seem more real. A shoe, anything, that could make me believe it's really Mary."

Moises arrived home later and I told him what we decided. In his inimitable manner, he made a difficult decision even harder when he said, "I would never do that to one of my family." But our painful decision was now made.

We now realized we needed a funeral director to make the necessary arrangements to bring Mary home. My only contact with a funeral home was in the early 1970's when Grandma Peg, my mother, lived with us in the final weeks of her bout with liver cancer. We pre-arranged with a funeral home in Schenectady to transport her down to New York City after she died. Vito died in Syracuse and he was buried out there.

We were still pondering this when Joan's husband, Mike, came up with an idea. "Pat, my parents' friends go to Gleason's. It's right next to St. John the Evangelist Church on Union Street. As a matter of fact, I went to school with Jim Gleason, one of the sons."

It was a good suggestion and I jumped at it. About an hour later, a tall young man, with an engaging smile, rang our doorbell. Jim Gleason knew most of Mike's brothers as he was a year behind him at St. John the Evangelist School. He blended in easily with our family, and I felt comfortable with him immediately.

Gerry told him as much as we knew at this time about Mary's death in Berkeley. "I spoke to the coroner's office and they gave me the name of a funeral home out in Oakland. I guess they're the ones you need to touch base with." That saved Jim from giving us a reference, as he often needs to with out-of-town deaths.

"Jim, we have decided to have Mary cremated. What do you think?" I asked a bit warily, perhaps still not fully comfortable with the decision.

"Mrs. Gioia, I think you have made a good decision. And I would recommend that you have the cremation done out there before bringing her home."

(In later years, Jim shared with me that when he contacted the Grant Miller Mortuary in Oakland, they were relieved to learn we had already decided on cremation. They told him there was no way a viewing could be held with the condition Mary's body was in. We had made the right decision after all.)

Then Jim asked, "Have you thought of where you want to bury the cremains?"

He admitted that he never talks a family out of holding on to the cremains, or, if they wish, scattering them. His gut feeling though was that there should be a place for a family to go to - to talk, to cry or to laugh, and to mourn their loved one. In other words, a burial site. It seemed such a bizarre conversation but by now, all of us were settling into the terrible realization that this is what we had to do for Mary. However, we did not have a burial plot.

"There's still one plot available down in Queens at Calvary Cemetery, where Grandma and Grandpa are buried," I offered.

Christine interjected, "Mom, how could we ever get to visit her if she's buried down there in New York City?"

Everyone agreed. Just then, Jim came to our rescue. "There are two cemeteries here I usually recommend to families. One is the Catholic cemetery, Most Holy Redeemer, on Route 7; the other is Park View, a nondenominational cemetery. Both are well-maintained and have beautiful park-like settings."

This sounded better and I asked, "Where's Park View Cemetery?"

"Off Fehr Avenue, right across from Central Park."

We all agreed that might be where to look for a plot. We knew Mary always enjoyed Central Park and it was near home.

Jim agreed. "That's a good plan. I don't like to have to do the choosing. I tell people they should go and stand right at the very spot they think they want. That's how you know if it seems right."

We felt very comfortable with Jim by this time, so I recall the following conversation brought about some needed smiles, if not outright laughter.

I asked Jim, "Since burying cremains are smaller than burying a coffin, could I or someone else be buried in this same grave?"

Jim smiled. "Yes, you could. I'm not sure what the final number is that could be buried in one grave, but there definitely could be several persons' cremains."

We bantered about who might want to join Mary when their turn came, some of us serious, some not. Finally, someone spoke up, "But I'm not sure I want to be cremated."

"Okay, well then you'll have to be on top of us all!"

Jim still needed more information for the obituary he would send on to the Gazette newspaper. The Times Union also published Mary's obituary, probably written from information retrieved from several news articles.

Next Jim asked, "Have you thought about having a funeral Mass or service?"

Our minds hadn't advanced that far either so I said, "Well, I could try St. John the Baptist Church." In the '70s, Vito and I had been active parishioners there. I called their office but as it was Saturday, the pastor was not available. It seemed a Mass could not be scheduled for a few days. When I hung up, I felt pressured. We needed this information for the obituary.

Noticing my anxiety, Jim said, "Mrs. Gioia, we can arrange to have a memorial service right at our Funeral Home. It could be held Tuesday if that's what you want. We have many of them and under the circumstances, it may be the best way to go."

"Okay, that sounds good," another weight now lifted from my weary shoulders. "If it's in Monday's paper, that should be enough time to let folks know." I thought too, perhaps Mary would be back home by then.

Jim proceeded to show us sample memorial cards. None grabbed our attention. We couldn't picture Mary's name on one of these religious cards, similar to the many her Grandma Peg kept in her prayer book. Mary's death was different. She didn't die from a fatal disease nor had she attained a ripe old age. Her young life was violently ended.

Rob now came up with a great idea. "Mom, why don't we design our own card? We could use the words Mary wrote on the back of her envelope with your letter. Remember?"

Yes, I remembered the words Mary wrote across the envelope flap. "All I leave behind me is only what I've found..." When I first read this, I admit I was puzzled. Then when I learned of her death, it almost sounded prophetic. Rob blew that notion when he told me these were words from "China Doll," a Grateful Dead song. We all agreed this was the perfect quote for her card. It may not have been prophetic but they were her final words to all of us.

We discussed what else should be on the card. Her name, Mary Regina Gioia, with no years of life. That would be too painful to see recorded on paper.

Gerry spoke up: "I've another idea. Why don't we duplicate the rose Mary drew for our wedding booklet on the card? It would make it more personal and really represent Mary."

We agreed. That rose was an appropriate symbol of our Mary's innocence and beauty. She originally drew it for a thank you note she left for Margie's parents. On a family visit to Baltimore, when most of us were deciding on the day's schedule, Mary sat back in a bedroom sketching the rose on the notepaper. It was a charming drawing, elegant in its simplicity. Margie and Gerry asked Mary to reproduce it for their wedding booklet. I recall Mary' surprise when asked, but she also felt honored by their request.

Once we agreed upon the memorial card, a friend of mine designed its final form. Although not ready to be given out at the memorial service, we sent them afterwards.

Jim still had another question: "Do you want to designate a charity in lieu of flowers in the obituary? Most families decide where contributions can be sent."

More discussion, more ideas tossed about. Everyone had input. We were becoming good at reaching these joint decisions, hard as they were. Since Mary did not die from cancer, heart disease or other malady, we needed to think outside the box of the usual list of charities.

Chris, recalling her birthday sister, said, "Remember how Mary loved to doodle and sketch; she was always drawing. How many pictures of that cat, Garfield, or Jerry Garcia, or roses did she draw?"

I said, "Yes, when I came over to your house on Mother's Day, Joan, the last one I'll ever have with her, there she was, perched on the couch, pad on her lap, sketching away. You're right, Chris; she loved to draw."

Other ideas came fast. Patrick offered his, "Remember she also loved music, especially the Dead." He would know; he was a Grateful Dead fan too.

I added Mary had begun to appreciate classical music also. When she worked in Lake George, one of her friends listened to a lot of classical music; she actually grew to like it.

Lawr, as he listened to everyone, summarized our thoughts. "Okay, I guess we can say Mary's major interests were art and music. Yes, even her baking resembled works of art. Hey, Ger, remember that Gingerbread House she baked?"

We chuckled recalling the time Mary made a gingerbread house. After baking, but before putting it together, she spread the pieces on the pass-through shelf in the kitchen. When Gerry walked by this tempting display, not realizing what they were, he picked one up and ate it. Later, Mary exclaimed, "Gerry, you ate the door!"

At this point, someone suggested that the Schenectady Arts Council might be the right choice as it would include both art and music. Besides, contributions would help Mary's hometown. It was decided. We told Jim to list the Schenectady Arts Council for memorial contributions.

Jim now had all the information he needed so he took leave of us for the day.

5

THE MEDIA ENTERS

News of Mary's murder traveled quickly. Friends and neighbors migrated to our house. John Principe was one of the first on the scene. He sat and talked to the family for several hours. John and his family were good friends since they moved to Schenectady and he opened up his dentistry practice. He was Dan's godfather. With seven children of his own, John knew well the terrible pain mine now experienced. Since their own father was gone, my family could pour their hearts out to John.

Many people stopped by to offer condolences. I recall Pat Jensen's visit. She was Lawr's close friend, Chris' mother. Her daughter, Linda, was killed in a local drunk driving crash a few years before. Lawr was terribly upset by her death, as Linda had been a good friend of his too. They often spent time together when they both attended college in New York City. I remember how angry Lawr became when a radio news story implied Linda was driving when the car crashed. The truth came out later that she was a passenger and was thrown from the car and killed. Sadly, the Jensens never received justice for Linda in their several court cases. Could we be on the same path?

Pat now tried to comfort me. She sat next to me on the living room sofa. One grieving mother to another. Only someone who has experienced the violent death of a loved one can actually know what it's like. Pat shared a poem with me that night which helped her and her husband, Bob, with Linda's loss, and she hoped it would do the same for me.

At this moment, my longtime friend, Doris Aiken,

36

appeared at the front door. She had not heard the news on the television or radio, but Pat Jensen called her. She knew Doris and I were friends for many years. Doris ran over to me, hugging me, "Pat I can't believe it. What happened?"

Doris and I met in 1972 during the George McGovern Presidential campaign. She and her husband, Bill, founded RID (Remove Intoxicated Drivers), a grass-roots anti-drunken driving organization in Schenectady in 1978. RID is now a national organization dedicated to educating the public, changing laws and serving victims and families of drunken driving crashes. Doris recruited me as Treasurer and a Charter Board Member in RID's early years. Doris knew Mary quite well as she lived at the Aiken's house for several months while a student at Schenectady Community College. Now she stood before me, crying and begging to know what happened.

I told Doris the little we knew about Mary's murder. Doris, with a long history of dealing with the media and helping victims, offered us some sage advice: "Choose someone in the family to be the official spokesperson. It's better to filter all remarks through one person." Gerry appeared to be the unanimous choice. He started to speak for all of us already.

Now the local media picked up on the story. Since CNN had been at the scene when Mary's body was brought to shore at the Berkeley Marina, the news quickly spread across the country. Local newspapers called for our comments. We said little at first because we did not know the full details and heeded the warning by the Berkeley police not to talk about the case. Television crews were soon at our doorstep.

A few days later, a friend living out in Berkeley sent me news clips from the California papers. The Oakland Tribune printed a short piece on Saturday, August 17th, when Mary's body was found. On Sunday, a longer story appeared because a second body (not yet identified) was discovered "submerged in 10 feet of water about 32 feet from shore." The article reported that Mark Garcia, the police spokesman, spoke to Harry Shorman, the so-called founder of Rainbow Village. Shorman said the man who was found had lived there about a week and Mary had stayed only the last two days. He and some of the other residents were fearful this incident would give the "controversial group of car dwellers bad publicity," and the residents were waiting for the police to solve the case and "for justice to be done." Weren't we all!

By Monday, the 19th, our local papers had the story. The <u>Times Union</u> quoted the California police who said Mary and Greg were "Grateful Dead devotees who lived in Rainbow Village, a commune near the Berkeley Marina, and trailed the rock group throughout the country attending 'concert after concert.'" <u>The Gazette,</u> also quoted Garcia, saying Mary and Greg had "been following the band." He also said that they had "a considerable amount of evidence. We may be able to solve it in a relatively short time."

We were angry when we read these accounts. No one asked us about Mary's reason for being in California. Yet the newspapers announced to the world that Mary had been "following the Grateful Dead rock band throughout California." How did they know? Mary was out there for only six weeks and at the commune for one night, the night before she was murdered. Why were we angry? Was it because we feared people would assume the wrong things about Mary? That this conduct was somehow not respectable? Out at the trial, some months later, one of the police officers admitted to me that when he was younger, he traveled from California to New Jersey with friends to hear a then popular band. He smiled impishly when he told me how they had spent a night huddled under the boardwalk in Atlantic City, just narrowly escaping the local police out searching for vagrants.

When I opened <u>The Gazette</u> that morning, I was shocked to see Mary's photo accompanying their story, "Murder of Niskayuna Woman Under Investigation in Calif." How eerie to see your daughter in the paper with such a caption! Mary seemed to stare out at us. When I first looked at it, I screamed "Where did they get that picture?" I never saw it before. I learned later it was her senior yearbook photo, and the media must have obtained it from the high school. Mary never ordered any copies of the photo. She probably did not like it and I could see why. She appeared much too serious, no smile, mouth closed tight to hide her braces. As I looked at it, I thought I saw a haunting expression on her face. She seemed to say, "Why? Why did this happen to me, Mom? I wasn't doing anything wrong. You know that. I was just being me."

Mary had a dream. She wanted to work out west. Don't we all have dreams—fantasies of where we want to go, what we want to do? Some of her friends had gone to Oregon, California, and Colorado, where Mary planned to go later that summer. At Gerry's wedding in May, Mary had a long, serious conversation with one of Gerry's friends about the West Coast where he had spent some time. He told me later Mary sounded so excited about going west and trying out her wings.

Gerry was quoted in both stories, disputing the reports that Mary was following the Grateful Dead as the reason she was out there. He said, "Mary was a Grateful Dead fan and she's attended concerts and some of her friends are Grateful Dead fans. But she didn't go out to California to follow the Grateful Dead." He described his sister: "She was a sweet, trusting, loving young lady who wouldn't hurt anyone. She had a great interest in the arts. She was a good artist and loved sketching and was a good cook and chef. She was very talented in putting together specialized foods."

How hard it must have been for him to try to tell the world the true story of his little sister. But he certainly did capture her in that quote.

Lawr also helped with the media. He took the call from The Knickerbocker News. "'There was no problem at all,' Larry Gioia, her 28-year-old brother, said Sunday night as he stood on the front porch of the family's two-story Cornelius Street home, 'It's a very sudden thing.'"

Again, after hearing the conjecture that Mary was traveling around the country following the Grateful Dead, Lawr said, "She was a fan of theirs, yes, but as far as following the group around—no. The truth is, she got a ride out to California with friends and she was working there."

Mary had driven out to California with a male friend, also a Grateful Dead follower. His mother owned a restaurant in southern California. For her ride out west, Mary worked in the restaurant for a few days—payback for the trip.

In the same Knickerbocker News article, Gerry mentioned the letter Mary had sent me. "She was happy. The letter just talked about getting jobs, so she could settle down more permanently."

The media likes to put their own spin on stories. Witness

how the <u>San Francisco Chronicle</u> (August 19) titles their report, "'Deadheads' Had Been Lovers – Hunt for Clues in Berkeley Killings." It reads:

> *Police dogs sniffed the Berkeley dump yesterday for clues to the slayings of two young drifters whose devotion to the Grateful Dead rock group kindled a romance just days before their deaths.*
>
> *Two sets of drag marks lead to blood-spattered rocks on the bay shore along the dump, where the bodies of Mary Regina Gioia, 22, of Schenectady, N.Y. and her companion were pulled into the water early Friday morning. Each had been shot once in the right temple at close range with a large-caliber weapon.*

It further describes how a State Department of Emergency Services boat carrying a search dog, tried to pick up the scent of the murder weapon and the killer's trail in the waters near the bay shoreline. At the trial, one of the policemen told me that the dog just leapt out of the boat into the water at the spot where Greg was buried. It had picked up the scent from the blood on the rocks.

The article continues:

> *The pair was last seen alive at 1:30 a.m. Friday as they sat together along an inlet of the bay, several hundred yards from the village entrance, police said. About an hour later, a resident of the village heard two sounds that could have been gunshots.*
>
> *Police Inspector Dan Wolke declined to speculate on the physical evidence or on information obtained from Rainbow Village residents and from other Deadheads. However, residents have given police at least two possible keys to the case: A 44-caliber weapon reported missing on Friday and a party that apparently involved an argument.*
>
> *The victims had been part of a small beer-drinking gathering that began Thursday night near*

the entrance to the village. Two men who identified themselves as village residents said the party involved five people—the victims, two other visitors and a resident, who was not identified.

Wolke would not give details of the party. But he said at one point, the two victims "walked off to be by themselves."

After the killings, a resident told police that a rifle he kept in his car inside the camp had been stolen.

According to accounts by residents, the man who reported his gun stolen had been with Gioia and Greg during the party but left them to buy more beer in Berkeley. When he returned, the residents said, the pair was gone.

It was painful to read these newspaper accounts. But they did provide us with information that was difficult to obtain since the murders occurred in another state across the country.

A local reporter, Joe Mahoney, from the <u>Times Union,</u> presented a more personal account of Mary and her place in the family. He wrote on Tuesday, August 20th ,

To her relatives, it was the most incongruous ending to a life that for 22 years, had been concerned with things such as art and peace and a healthy environment.

"Her having a connection with a homicide is so unbelievable" Jerry Gioia, one of the victim's brothers, said Monday as he and other grieving family members prepared for a memorial service for the slain woman today at the Gleason Funeral Home in Schenectady.

"She was a kid who was very interested in social concerns," the brother said. He noted that, several months ago, Mary participated in a peaceful protest march with her mother, Patricia Gioia-Riano, outside the Seneca Falls Army Depot, where the military is believed to keep stockpiles of nuclear weapons.

"She was interested in people's welfare," he added. *"Our family looks at that as a very positive thing."*

Gerry challenged the reason given by some newspaper accounts for Mary having gone to California.

"She wasn't romping around the country, that wasn't the case. Mary was a fan of theirs (Grateful Dead) and attended a lot of their concerts. That was one of her interests, and she had many other interests. She was interested in weaving. She could sketch and do watercolors. She was a free spirit in the sense that she followed her own mind. She loved to go out and do things for herself."

And regarding the purported romance with Greg, Gerry said his sister "had made no mention of the man who was slain with her in recent letters and telephone calls to family members."

I think we made a good choice of family spokesman when we chose her brother.

We now knew the name of the young man murdered with Mary - Greg Kniffin. His father, David Kniffin, of Wilton, Connecticut, went out to California to identify him. Greg, too, had been shot in the head with a large caliber weapon.

Several days after Mary and Greg had been recovered, divers from the Berkeley Police Underwater Search and Rescue Team continued to look for additional clues. Dogs, provided by the California Rescue Dog Association, were used in boats and along the shoreline to track any human scent in case there were additional victims. They were also looking to find the murder weapon. The police spokesman said no new evidence was discovered.

6

CHANNEL SIX INTERVIEW

We grew tired of being cooped up in the house and wandered out to the front porch. A few of my sons' friends had arrived and several were on the porch swing. They tried to bolster up their spirits. We were not aware of the local television station photographing us, its truck parked down the road.

A Channel Six photographer soon came over to us and said, "If you don't want to be in the photo, I suggest you go inside."

We thanked him and took his heeding. We did not want to be photographed on the porch as the newest grieving family.

As we went inside, the phone was ringing. Gerry answered. It was Judy Sanders from Channel Six, a local CBS television affiliate. Judy, who often reported on local crime stories, wanted to do an exclusive—an interview with a family member. Gerry, not sure how we all would react to such a request, said he'd get back to her.

The porch incident helped us decide to get our own message out about Mary, on our terms. We would accept the request for the interview, but who would do it was now the question.

"Gerry, you've been the spokesman so far. Would you want to do it?" I asked. I felt it might be best to have a sibling speak.

Gerry put his arm around my shoulder and replied, "No, I think you should speak for Mary, Mom. You know we're all behind you."

Although I felt a little nervous, down deep, I knew I

could do it. After all, just a few years ago I had been a political candidate, meeting the public, giving a few speeches. That experience would help me now to make my most important speech, telling everyone about my daughter, Mary.

I called Judy, saying, "After talking it over with the family, we've decided to accept your offer to do an interview. I'll speak for the family and my daughter."

Judy thanked me and said she would be over later in the afternoon. Doing it at our home would provide a more personal setting. This had been Mary's home too. Judy then asked that we have some pictures of Mary available.

We still had only scattered pieces of information on the murder. The distance—3,000 miles between Schenectady and Berkeley—intensified our feelings of futility and helplessness. We were at the mercy of the police out there to feed us information. All we could do was wait to hear if an arrest was made. In the meantime, we were determined to keep a positive portrayal of Mary before the public.

We searched for a photo of Mary. It wasn't easy. Which one should we use? We wanted to show her beauty, her innocence and her place in the family.

We chose one that was taken several years before that hung on our living room wall. It seemed to portray Mary's innocence; her wide-open hazel eyes stared out at us. Her unblemished pale complexion sharply contrasted with her dark curly hair. She looked serious with her mouth closed tight to conceal braces. A favorite red tartan vest partially covered a white button-down shirt.

Now that we had selected the photo, we wanted to show Mary's artistic talent. That was easy as we quickly located a sketch of an arrangement of flowers, her favorite red roses dominating. Rob placed the photo, with the drawing next to it, in a brown frame.

A more difficult assignment was to find a photo of Mary and me together that Judy had requested. After scouring my box of photos, we discovered one taken several years back at my graduation from Empire State College. In the photo, Mary appeared somewhat shy, in contrast to me, who had a look of silent triumph at my accomplishment.

Judy Sanders arrived at the house in mid-afternoon, her

photographer in tow. She introduced herself, but, of course, we had seen her many times on our television screen. After settling in, she said, "Okay, Mrs. Gioia, why don't you tell us about your daughter, Mary."

I forced a smile and looked straight into the camera and said:

> *Mary was a loving person; she loved everyone in the family. Her last letter was filled with love and hope and her desire for getting her job in California.*

I was determined to get that point out—she was out there to find a job.

Sanders, standing in front of the house continued,

> *Mary's mother received that letter last Friday, the night the police came to notify her that her 22-year old daughter was dead. Mary was found with a male companion in the Berkeley, California Marina. Both had a single gun shot to the head. Berkeley police say that for two days Mary had lived at Rainbow Village, a community or commune of buses and vans."*

The spot near the rocky shore where Mary was found flashed on the screen. Divers were shown entering the water. Scenes of Rainbow Village displayed the buses parked outside the fence, a little girl standing next to her father, and a Grateful Dead bumper sticker on a car. Sanders continued,

> *Earlier reports said Mary was a devoted follower of the Grateful Dead. Her mother said she thinks she attended the June concert in SPAC but she was not a devotee. Mary's mother said she did not go to California to follow the Grateful Dead, although she was a fan of theirs. She was not a so-called Deadhead, and she was not involved in drugs.*

At that point, I emphasized that what had been said up to now in the media is not true.

I think some of the things said about Mary, about being a Deadhead, or following the Grateful Dead out to California, are untrue. I know they are untrue.

Sanders continued with more facts about Mary noting she was a 1981 graduate of Niskayuna High School, and adding,

She had a degree in culinary arts from Schenectady Community College and specialized in artistic pastries, like this Easter basket.

At this point, the Easter basket Mary made several years ago, complete with several colored eggs, was shown.

Her mother describes her as industrious and trusting.

With a smile, I described Mary:

In the language of the vernacular, she was laid-back. She was a very special free spirit, we might call her. But let me also say that Mary was industrious. Never did she sit around and not have a job.

Now a portion of a 1979 Mother's Day story Channel Six did on our family was inserted into the interview. It pictured Mary standing at the stove, stirring food and smiling. I'm shown preparing vegetables at the sink, and Dan, grinning widely, walks past his brother, Patrick, also preparing food at the counter. We looked like a good family team, everyone working together.

(A former intern in my office worked at Channel Six and was assigned to find a novel or unusual family for a Mother's Day segment. At the time, I was a single mother with a number of children. The station seized that concept, and there we were!)

Judy Sanders ended the interview, recalling that the Mother's Day story had closed with a photograph of the card Mary had given me that day with a lovely bouquet of flowers. She had written, "Mom, I hope you have a great day. Love ya, Mary."

We huddled together in the living room later that night, awaiting the airing of the interview. Would it present Mary as we wanted her to be known? As we watched, we all shed tears, especially when we saw Mary, so alive, so vibrant in that tape. When the news report ended, we were sure that the public now had a better picture of Mary and why she went to California.

Shortly before the interview aired, my brother, Marty, my only sibling, arrived from Florida. When he heard of Mary's death, he made arrangements for his young seven-year old son, Marty Jan, to stay with his daughter, Kathleen, so he could come up to New York to be with us. He knew how important it was for me—and him—to be together at this time.

7

TUESDAY – THE MEMORIAL SERVICE

August 20, 1985 - On this day we publicly celebrated Mary Regina's life and mourned her death. The Memorial Service took place at 11 am at the Gleason Funeral Home.

I woke up early that morning. For the last few nights, I hadn't slept well. In the first days after I learned about Mary's murder, I toughed it out, grabbed a few winks at night and survived on nervous energy. My mind continually had thoughts of Mary and what she suffered at the hands of that maniac who killed her.

Jim Gleason was my savior. He made all arrangements for the service. The only relatives to attend were our immediate family – Mary's two sisters and five brothers – and their life partners. Moises and my brother, Marty, were there too. No other extended family. I had not contacted any except Marty; most lived a distance away and everything had happened so quickly.

After breakfast, all of us staying at the house headed down to Gleason's. Located directly across from Union College on Union Street, it is a large two-story, red brick building, with windowed gables on the roof. White pillars flank the front. One by one, the rest of the family arrived, all somber and a bit anxious. For most of them, a wake was a new experience. Several attended their grandparents' funerals, but not all. Some had been too young, or away at school.

Jim Gleason met us at the door. We spoke for a few moments, and he reassured me that everything was in order for the service. I thanked him and handed him Mary's photo. "We put this together yesterday for the Channel Six interview."

"Yes, I saw it, Mrs. Gioia. I thought it went well, and I think you explained in no uncertain terms why Mary was in California."

Jim took the photo and placed it on a wooden pedestal next to several floral arrangements. Mary's cremains hadn't arrived from California so her photo had to suffice. Each time I glanced over, tears welled up. I wanted to call out to her, "What are you doing here? It didn't really happen, did it?"

Bertrand Fay, our long-time priest friend, conducted the Memorial. Mary's dad, Vito, and I knew Bert since he was a young curate at St. Helen's Church in the early 1960's. Vito and he became close friends, both working for long-awaited change within the Church. Bert had baptized Mary so it was fitting that he now conduct the final service for her in this life.

In his years at St. Helen's, Bert was almost a member of our family. Our home was just around the corner so he often wandered over to talk, sometimes playing a few tunes on our old piano. Bert had been a priest advisor for the parish Christian Family Movement (CFM) group, in which Vito and I were quite involved.

I tried desperately to focus on Bert's homily, but found my thoughts overwhelmed by the horrible image of Mary in her last moments. Bert spoke of Mary's soul's immediate transcendence in the presence of Christ and his Holy Mother, but I was stuck in a painful mortal world.

When Bert finished his homily, Robert stood up from his seat. He walked to the front of the room, guitar in hand. It took me by surprise. I was not aware of what he was about to do.

He said, "Hi, everyone. I'm Rob, Mary's brother. This morning when I woke up in her room at my sister, Joan's house, I found a song sheet she had framed and hung on her wall." Then, he looked over at her photo on the pedestal and said, "Mary, this one is for you."

Robert began to strum his guitar. The chords vibrated in the crowded room of friends who had come to say goodbye to Mary. His voice quivered as he started to sing the words to "Ripple," a Grateful Dead tune. With each verse, his voice grew stronger. I will always remember the courage and grace Robert displayed as he stood by Mary's picture, playing his guitar, singing, and stealing a look at her. There was not a dry eye in the room as he sang this dedication to his sister.

The verses of "Ripple" were haunting, almost foreboding.

RIPPLE

If my words did glow with the gold of sunshine
And my tunes were played on the harp un-strung
Would you hear my voice come through the music?
Would you hold it near, as it was your own?
It's a hand me down, the thoughts are broken;
Perhaps they're better left unsung.
I don't know, don't really care.
Let there be songs to fill the air.
Ripple in still water, when there is no pebble tossed,
Nor wind to blow; Reach out your hand
If your cup be empty, if your cup is full, may it be again.
Let it be known, there is a fountain—that was not made
by the hands of men.
There is a road, no simple highway, between the dawn and
the dark of night.
And if you go, no one may follow
That path is for your steps alone.
Ripple in still water, when there is no pebble tossed, nor
wind to blow
You who choose to lead must follow,
But if you fall, you fall alone.
If you should stand, then who's to guide you?
If I knew the way, I would take you home.

When the service was over, I stood up at my seat, saying, "Thank you all for being here and for the love and support you have shown to me and my family. We couldn't do it without you."

After this, we stayed and mingled with the long line of those who had come.We shook hands, hugged and cried. Neighbors, friends, work colleagues, political buddies, my children's friends, their parents, Mary's friends, the list went on and on of those who attended. Doris and Bill Aiken had to sit in the outer room, as the room where the service was held was filled with people and a tremendous outpouring of love.

We left Gleason's and headed back to the house. On the way home, I asked Robert about his choice of the song, "Ripple." He explained,

> Brenda and I were staying at Joan's, in Amanda's room, on a mattress on the floor. I woke up early and began to go through some of Mary's things that were in the room. I spotted a crystal heart box I gave her. It was probably a trade show sample when I worked for Leonard Silver. I caught a whiff of patchouli from it. Then I went through some albums she had. I think some were Gerry's from the '60s. I spotted a picture of her from her "cleaning days" up in Lake George with some of her friends, all holding brooms. I put it in my wallet.

I was glad to learn Rob had helped himself to some of Mary's things. I'm sure she would like to know a part of her had gone with him. Then I asked, "Is that where you found the song sheet for Ripple?"

> Yeah, she had this wrinkled, kind of pink colored sheet with the words, one that they give out at the Dead concerts. It was glued on to a heavier backing and in a dark gold frame. I guess I thought she might like that one, especially since she had hung it on her wall."

"But why did you do a solo, since Patrick also plays the guitar?"

> Patrick didn't know the song. And since Joan's house was packed with people, I went out in the car and practiced. So I was ready when I got over to Gleason's.

Once home we found a feast and reception prepared for us by our many close neighbors and friends. Platters of appetizing food, cold and hot entrees, salads, rolls, and many delicious desserts appeared on every available surface in the kitchen and dining room. The house and backyard had tables set up and over-flowed with neighbors, friends and those of Mary's sisters and brothers. Groups of people, young and old, were talking and smiling as they recalled the light that was Mary. No one would ever suspect by glancing at them that it was such a sad occasion. It was a time to accept expressions of sympathy. It was a time to talk about Mary with the people who knew and loved her

As I greeted visitors to our home, I felt a strange sensa-tion in my right cheek, similar to a toothache. It was not overly severe, but nagging. I hadn't felt it earlier in the day. It didn't last very long. As I thought about it, I realized that the pain I experi-enced was in almost the identical spot on Mary where she was shot. Could this have been sympathetic pain I experienced? Or perhaps it was a sign from Mary that she was there with us.

8

THE NEXT FEW DAYS

The Memorial was over but more hard tasks lie ahead. On Wednesday we had to find a burial place for Mary. Oh, God, how do you do that? In my mind I heard repeated: children are supposed to bury their parents, not the other way. But I felt stronger today. The love and compassion family and friends showered on us yesterday boosted my spirits. I would make it through the next hurdle. With my coffee cup in hand and these thoughts racing through my mind, Joan flew in the back door. "Okay, who's going with us, Mom?" When something needed to be done, you could count on Joan. Her high energy level kept us on track now.

"Gerry and Margie, you and me."

"Okay, guys, let's move it."

They just finished breakfast and brought their dishes over to the sink. Margie had been officially in our family for only a few months but already was involved with our concerns. She would go along to support Gerry. From a family of five siblings, she knew how much he was hurting. Margie had a physical disability of her own that she handled with true grace. She had a leg removed because of cancer about five years before. Except for walking at a slightly slower gait, it was not obvious, and all of us quickly forgot about it. She loved Mary as a sister and now would accompany us to find a burial place for her.

As the four of us got into Joan's car, Gerry reflected on the last few days, "I know it's going to take a lifetime to realize Mary is really gone, but having everyone here with us yesterday made it

a little easier. I still can't believe how many of my buddies came."
He was right. All of the kids had so many friends who, when they
heard about Mary, came to console them.

We were thankful the weather cooperated; it was sunny
but hot. Rain would have really drowned our spirits. Driving
along Fehr Avenue, we soon passed the entrance to Schenectady's
Central Park. My mind flashed to the many happy times we had
there when the children were young. Continuing on, we passed
the baseball fields on the right. The entrance to the cemetery
appeared to our left. Tall green hedges almost hid the stone pillars
marking the entranceway. We saw the dark metal sign bearing the
name, "Park View." The roadway into the cemetery widened as we
drove up to the administration building. The gray stone building
resembled a storybook gingerbread house. We parked our car and
entered through the dark hardwood doors, still anxious, not
knowing what to expect. A tall, pleasant-looking woman quickly
greeted us. "Can I help you?"

Blurting out, "We have to find a burial spot for my daughter," I could feel the tears filling my eyes.

The woman quickly asked us to sit down. She knew we
were all on the verge of tears. It's probably a daily occurrence for
her, grieving relatives coming to select a grave.

Gerry spoke up and explained briefly what had happened
to Mary. I was amazed he could tell this horrible story in so few
words and so gently. "Jim Gleason suggested we look at Park
View for a grave site."

"I'm so sorry to hear about your daughter and your sister.
Let me drive and show you what's available here."

We left the building and all climbed into our guide's
large, comfortable black automobile. As she drove, she pointed
out the many sections of Park View. Most paths were lined with
tall green trees that hugged the roadway. It was larger than I imagined, having seen it only driving past on Fehr Avenue.

Joan tried to keep the conversation light and said, "It
seems so peaceful. I'm glad we're looking here."

Yes, I too felt the serenity. It was not at all like Calvary
Cemetery where Mom and Dad were buried. There, headstones
upon headstones are lined up as far as the eye can see. There
were clusters of graves in some areas here too but it didn't seem
crowded. Many were adorned with plantings and flowers. I liked

that; we'd be able to bring flowers to Mary here. Oh, how she loved flowers! It still seemed so surreal that I was there to pick out her grave.

Our guide continued to show us available sites. None seemed right. At this point, I started to laugh. Joan, wondering if I had finally cracked, said, "Mom, what's wrong?"

"Does anyone remember the television show, 'The Odd Couple'? In one episode Felix and Oscar went to a cemetery to choose a plot for Felix. What we're doing now reminded me of it. Each spot they looked at had some drawback. Felix would lie down in the grass to test it out and try to imagine being buried there."

I laughed again, "One spot he looked at was right under a tree. As he lay there on the grass, all he could think of were the birds sending their droppings down - right on top of him. He jumped up, horrified. He wasn't going to choose that spot either. Sorry, if I worried you. Our search for the perfect grave site here, made me think of that."

Everyone laughed, and we realized we could even find some humor in this dismal task. Just as we approached the section near the administration building, we spied an area we liked. It was not crowded with graves, and there was a tree at the top of this small bluff.

Gerry asked quickly, "Is anything available up there?"

"As a matter of fact, there are a few openings right up near the tree. Do you want to go look?"

We certainly did. After we emerged from the car, we walked up the grassy knoll to the area near the young maple tree. We stepped over inlaid stones in the grass, bearing names of men and women who had once lived among us. Small evergreen bushes sprouted up sporadically along our path planted by relatives of the deceased. Our guide pointed out an available site near the tree. It seemed just about what we were looking for.

As we stood there, under the tree, Gerry said decisively, "This looks good. I think Mary would love this place." He knew his sister, and we agreed; this would be where we would bury our Mary.

Our guide, pleased we had finally found a site, led us back to the building to fill out the necessary papers. After that, we climbed back in Joan's car, relieved that this piece was over. We headed over to K & A Memorials on State Street. They had been recommended also by Jim Gleason. We faced another difficult assignment, which we could never have imagined. We needed to choose a headstone for Mary's grave. We looked at several samples and quickly decided we didn't want those tall or showy ones. We saw some at the cemetery and felt they would definitely not do for Mary. Finally, we selected a modest-sized gray stone that would rise at a slight angle from the ground. And it had ample room for several names and dates.

"GIOIA," would be engraved across the stone. The next line would read, "Mary Regina 1962 – 1985." We chose a large rose, enclosed in a circle, to be engraved next to her name, symbolizing our Gioia Rose. We were promised that the headstone would be placed at the grave in a few months. As we headed home, we realized we had made some difficult, but necessary, choices today.

– – –

It's Friday…one week since we learned of Mary's murder. It was one of the longest weeks of my life. Each day had seen its own challenge. Today, we would perform our last physical act for Mary. We would bury her. I worried that her cremains would not arrive in time for Bert Fay to perform the committal service, as he was preparing to leave town. At last, Jim Gleason called to say they were here from California.

Naturally, I felt relieved but how do you possibly relate to something like this? I once had a child, a beautiful child, and now all that remains of her are cremains! And they will soon be buried in the ground. I thanked God for helping us negotiate through all the unspeakable tasks that needed to be done without completely losing our sanity.

We gathered in the kitchen before we headed over to the cemetery. It was another hot and sunny day. Everyone looked piqued and tired. It had been a long, hard, heartbreaking time for everyone. Lawr, Robert and Patrick sat on the front porch swing practicing the song that we would bury Mary to: "Forever Young." Strains of the music and words filtered in. *May your heart always be joyful. May a song always be sung. May you stay Forever Young.*

We sat around, making small talk, waiting for Bert Fay to

arrive. We didn't know just what to expect when we got to Park View. This was the first time most of the family had been to a burial ceremony. When Bert arrived, we left for the cemetery.

With our cars parked on the roadway closest to the site, we trooped up the slight hill to the tree near the gravesite we had chosen. We met a few others who had already arrived. We were a small crowd, but those closest to Mary, were there. All of our family, except Mary Ann who had gone home for her job; Mark Sgarlata and John Fiorillo, Mary's two faithful boyfriends; my longtime friend, Fran Leary; a few of Gerry's friends; and Joan's two brothers-in-law, Joey and Rick Celentano, were at the grave. Jim Gleason and his father, Thomas Gleason, the founder of the Funeral Home, waited for us at the top of the hill.

We gathered around the tree, next to the spot where Mary would be buried. Nobody spoke but a feeling of anxiety pervaded the air. Then Bert began the service. Again, I felt disconnected from the words, though comforted by his presence.

When Bert finished his homily, Robert, Lawr and Patrick began to strum the haunting melody of "Forever Young" on their guitars. Lawr passed out copies of the words to us so we could follow along. As he did, he said, "When I heard Mary was dead, I tried to keep from going crazy. I couldn't believe it. She couldn't be! Then I found this song. I think it says what we all feel about her."

We joined in singing the beautiful lyrics dedicated to our "Forever Young" Mary.

Forever Young
By Bob Dylan

May God bless and keep you always,
May your wishes all come true,
May you always do for others
And let others do for you.
May you build a ladder to the stars
And climb on every rung,
May you stay forever young,
Forever young, forever young,
May you stay forever young.

May you grow up to be righteous,
May you grow up to be true,
May you always know the truth
And see the lights surrounding you.
May you always be courageous,
Stand upright and be strong,
May you stay forever young,
Forever young, forever young,
May you stay forever young.

May your hands always be busy,
May your feet always be swift,
May you have a strong foundation
When the winds of changes shift.
May your heart always be joyful,
May your song always be sung,
May you stay forever young.
Forever young, forever young,
May you stay forever young.

When we finished singing, Robert peeled off the small sheet of paper he had taped to his guitar. He walked over to the urn and, with tears falling, taped it to the urn. A bit of us would be forever with Mary.

9

MARY REGINA – PART ONE

Mary Regina arrived in our family at 4:40 p.m. on December 20, 1962. The seventh child, third girl, she was our smallest baby, weighing 6lbs., 2 oz. at birth. Our family doctor, Stephen Grey, determined that this baby should arrive before Christmas, shooed me off to St. Clare's Hospital early that morning to begin the process. The other children enjoyed a little vacation from home, and each other, as they were pared off with friends for a few days. December 20th was also Christine's birthday so we celebrated with an early birthday cake for her the night before. Thanks to her substitute family, she had a second birthday cake too. But, by far, her most special birthday gift that year was her new little sister. Although there were eight years between them, Christine and Mary, whenever possible, celebrated their birthdays together. Birthday sisters.

Little Mary was very much welcomed, especially by Joan and Christine. After four brothers in a row, they were delighted with a little sister. A cute and cuddly baby, Mary had big hazel eyes and curly brown hair that they loved to brush and comb and style in so many ways. They agreed she was much more fun than any doll because she could walk, talk and even giggle. Christine said she didn't need a Barbie, she had Mary.

Born close to Christmas, Mary's father and I chose to honor the Mother of Jesus when naming our new little daughter. Her middle name, Regina, was also a tribute to Mary, the Queen of Heaven. But I will admit the name, Mary, had always been a favorite of mine. Simple and plain, to me was its charm. Not long home from the hospital, Mary was baptized at St. Helen's Church by our friend, Father Bertrand Fay, and Tom and Miriam Aery, good friends from our Christian Family Movement group, were godparents.

Shortly after her birth, we noticed Mary had a "lazy eye," not new to our family, as three of her siblings also had this condition. After numerous visits to Dr. Kennedy, the ophthalmologist, and a subsequent operation at about age three, her eyes were straightened. Mary wore glasses for many years. Her small pink or blue glasses, sometimes sliding down on her little nose, made her look even cuter, if that was possible.

Growing up, Mary was generally a happy child, although outwardly she appeared to be slightly shy or reserved. When her brother, Daniel, was born in 1966, she gave up her place as the baby in the family. Three years older, she now was a "big sister." She loved her little brother and he became her favorite doll. As the two youngest, they had a special relationship but there was also competition for the attention of their older sisters and brothers. It broke down into a separation of the sexes. Recognizing his athletic prowess early on, Dan's brothers, and some of their friends, groomed him to be an ace athlete, excelling in most sports, especially football. On the other hand, Joan and Christine took Mary under their wings. She loved spending time with them upstairs in their third-floor bedroom. It was there she learned about being a girl in the '70s, imitating much of what they did. She even copied Christine's cursive handwriting style, using large, neat and legible letters. It was hard sometimes to distinguish between them.

Mary and Dan retained that certain bond, as the two "last on the list, like Oliver Twist," to quote an old familiar saying in our family. And it continued, although it may have been hidden under the weight of time. Many years later, when Dan and his wife, Kelly, were expecting their first child, Dan telephoned me. It was close to Mary's anniversary, always a difficult time for all of us.

"Mom, guess what we are going to name the baby?"

I told him I couldn't imagine. I wasn't sure I wanted to hear either. Secretly I hoped it wasn't one of the very "mod," contemporary names he and Kelly had talked about.

"We're going to name her Erin Mary."

I couldn't speak for several minutes as I choked back tears. Finally, when I collected myself, I said, "Dan, it's such a beautiful name. Mary must be very happy with her little brother."

Mary loved her grandparents. She saw more of my parents, Grandma Peg and Grandpa Jack Malone, than Grandma Tess (Teresa Gioia, Vito's mother). In her prime, Grandma Peg would often hop on the Greyhound Bus and come up from New York City for a short visit. Sometimes Grandpa Jack would drive to Schenectady with her in his large, older-model automobile used for his house painting business.

In the summer of 1970, our house suddenly became crowded when my mother came up from New York City to stay with us. She had cancer with only a few months to live. Mary came to our rescue when she willingly gave up her bedroom on the second floor to her grandmother and came to us with a plan.

"Mom, I can stay in the basement playroom. You know that space right next to the laundry room. That can be my bedroom. I'll fix it up. It'll be fun and I won't have to be near Danny and Pat (Patrick) all the time!" She loved being able to be independent and away from those "pesky" brothers.

So she proceeded to set up her new room. She hung a rope starting at the doorway to the work side of the basement that housed our washing machine and dryer and workshop. The separator extended straight across the playroom. Next she hung colorful flowered sheets on the rope, sectioning off a sleeping area from the rest of the room. Since it was a temporary arrangement, she used a cot for her bed. An easy chair completed the area. Here in her own little bedroom, she seemed quite happy and content, enjoying her own special space. I'm sure her faithful pal, Gato, our cat, joined her there most nights. When her grandmother died, Mary moved back to the second floor, staying there until she eventually made her way up to the third floor, as her older sisters moved out.

When Grandma Peg died in November of 1970, Mary wrote about it in school:

> *Mary Gioia, March 3rd 1971*
> *My Saddest Day*
> *My saddest day was when my grandmoth-*

er died. She was very nice. Then one day she got very, very, very sick and died. Then my mother told me she died. And that was the end of my true story.
THE END.

Then Mary drew a headstone, which read "Margaret Malone died November 1st 1970," with two little flower plants on either side. Grandma Peg must have smiled at these words straight from her granddaughter's heart.

When Mary and her siblings were growing up, life seemed simpler, less structured than today. If there wasn't homework or chores, she had lots of free time to be herself. She had several close girlfriends. One friend, Elizabeth Gilbert—everyone called her Bodie—lived across the street. Her brothers and Mary's brothers were also good friends. Mary and Bodie remained bosom buddies until Bodie's family moved to Syracuse when it became a long-distance friendship. Years later, Bodie would write a touching victim's impact letter to the Judge.

> I'm writing to you in regard to my best friend Mary Gioia. Mary and I had been friends since I was six, she four.
>
> Mary was the sweetest little girl and she grew up to be not only beautiful, but also very kind, generous, and warm. I moved when I was nine, yet we always stayed in touch through all those years, by writing, visiting each other and even long distance phone calls.
>
> We got along great, always giggled and were always up to some mischief. Sometimes we'd play dolls, then we'd go off and climb trees with our brothers. I have two and she had 5. What fun we had...Believe me, a day does not go by without me thinking of her....
>
> All I can really say, is that I truly loved Mary and I cherish her in my heart always.
> Elizabeth

Reading Bodie's words, I can picture the two of them, running around with, or after, their brothers. It was an innocent time and they were innocent too.

Mary had other close friends: Theresa Hastings, Toni DeAngelo, Marjorie Leary, and Lise Stukey. When Lise moved to Florida, a highlight in Mary's early teen years was her visit to see her. Mary was there for several weeks, definitely unusual in our stay-near-to-the-base family. We celebrated with a small "welcome home" party when she returned. And it was a big surprise for us to see how mature she now acted—and looked—sporting a new short haircut.

Our family vacations began when we learned from friends about camping and the economies of tenting. On one of our trips back home from the Emerald Lake camping grounds in Vermont, we stopped at the Bennington Museum. This was a treat, at least for me, now finally squeezing a bit of culture into our ten days of living out of tents! However, this innocent side expedition almost turned into a financial disaster. Browsing near the Grandma Moses paintings, some of which were placed on the floor next to the wall, Mary accidentally knocked one over. The glass crashed, and Mary burst into tears. Now, what would happen? Her Dad left our name and address with the Museum so we could be notified of the cost to repair the damage. But perhaps the worst damage was to Mary as she was forced to endure continual taunting by her brothers. The Museum took it far less seriously and declined to charge us for the repair. They said they realized it was an innocent mistake. This incident remained part of family history and was always brought up whenever we passed that spot in Bennington.

School and learning proved more difficult for Mary than for most of her sisters and brothers. But she tried very hard and did her best. She expressed this in a note when she was nine:

> *Dear Mom and Dad: With conferences just around the corner, I want to let you know how I think things are going. Things are going pretty good but not bad. I think that I can do better than I am doing now. I will try to do it just a little better,and after that I can try even more. Your girl Mary.*

A parent can't ask for much more than that! And she kept her promise. She continued to try hard.

The next year, when she was ten years old, we attended a "Back to School Night." Mary left a note for us at her desk. It read:

>Dear Mom and Dad,
>When you come don't bother looking in my desk it might be messy but it might be clean. We got some games like the one in the back of the room. It has animals on the back bulletin board. That big cat back there looks like Gato doesn't it? But Gato has more stripes. Gato has the same kind of eyes right! Mean eyes right.
>Well I guess that's all.
>Your daughter, Mary

Gato! Oh, how Mary loved that tiger cat. When we first got her, and this was a great compromise by her father who didn't particularly like animals in the house, some of the older children were learning Spanish in school. So, Gato, meaning cat in that language, was the name chosen unanimously for our new cat. Mary had many photos of Gato in her album in all kinds of positions, eating, standing up and one with her carrying it in a straw basket. One of my favorites is Mary seated on our back porch, grasping Gato, who looks like it is about to leap out of her arms. Mary is smiling, just slightly; a broad smile might reveal her braces. Her brown hair appears at its curliest, forming little ringlets around her face. And if I look carefully, I think her shirt, partly hidden by Gato, has a symbol of her favorite band, The Grateful Dead. Gato remained a member of the family for many years until 1988, when she became sick and had to be put to sleep. It was a sad day for the Gioia's, as that funny little cat had been the center of many family memories and stories.

Before she went to California, Mary acquired her own cat. She and her friend, John, each had one. She named hers Samson; he named his Delilah. Mary was arranging for Joan to send Samson out to her in California, but, sadly, that never happened. When Mary was murdered, Joan couldn't bear to part with her cat so she kept Samson. One day, Joan arrived home from a dentist appointment and the neighbors told her Samson ran into the street and was killed by a passing car. Now Joan felt another connection with her sister had been wrenched from her.

Mary loved music but like many youngsters, she did not love to practice. She played the clarinet in grade school but gave it up after a few years. In her album, she kept a photo of herself in front of a music stand set up in her basement bedroom. Little blue glasses perched on her nose, she looked quite serious as she practiced her clarinet.

And for a while, too, she had an interest in learning to play the piano. Her sister, Joan, took lessons for several years. For Mary, it didn't last that long. This meant daily practicing. Her piano teacher, an older man and excellent instructor, had recently moved up to Schenectady from New York City. Undoubtedly, his other students were far more interested and faithful at practicing than Mary as one day, he telephoned me, saying, "Mrs. Gioia, I cannot teach Mary anymore. She's not a serious student, and I just don't have time for someone like that." While I was disappointed, I think Mary was relieved.

Mary dearly loved to sketch and draw. In her quieter moments, even as a youngster, she could be found with a sheet of paper, pencil or crayon in hand, happily drawing. I have a scrapbook filled with many cards she made for me for every Hallmark occasion. Drawing gave her a way to express her feelings. She drew many family scenes. One shows Dan and her sitting at the "pass-through" counter between our kitchen and dining room. A box reading, "Snap, Crackle, Pop" and a carton reading "Milk" sit on the counter. Mary is seated on a brown bench, similar to the one we actually had at the pass-through. With a pencil in hand, she is sketching Dan who is sitting across the counter from her. He, too, is drawing a picture of her. Dan has straight black hair and black-rimmed eyeglasses like the ones he actually wore. Above his head is a small round halo, bearing the words, "Means Angel," perhaps written with a bit of sarcasm!

From an early age, Mary held down several after-school jobs to earn money. She wanted to follow in her brothers' footsteps and be a newspaper carrier for the Gazette, but, at the time, it didn't have morning routes for girls. Instead, she had an afternoon route for a short while with the Knickerbocker News. Later, she helped her brother, Patrick, collect from his customers, a job he did not favor. She was very good at this, keeping accurate records for him.

When older and able to have a better-paying job, Mary was a waitress at the Friendly's Restaurant on Upper Union Street. Her uniform, a blue and white checkered dress, was continually in the washing machine. Mary worked some afternoons on school days and on the weekends. Combined with babysitting jobs in the neighborhood, she always had spending money.

During her last two years in high school, Mary once again followed the lead of her sister, Christine. She enrolled in the BOCES (Board of Cooperative Educational Services) program for food services. Chef Andy was her instructor, as he was for Christine. The program was a half-day afternoon session, following a morning of academic subjects at Niskayuna High School. Mary thrived in this arrangement and it seemed to suit her better than a strictly academic curriculum. It also prepared her to discover what she wanted to do after high school

Mary's father, Vito, moved to Syracuse shortly after our divorce in 1975. Mary and Dan went out to visit him several times, and it was often coupled with a visit to her friend, Bodie. Mary looked forward to seeing her Dad at his new home or on his frequent visits back to Schenectady. He and Mary had a special relationship. For several years, Vito owned and directed an educational franchise, Learning Foundations, which helped youngsters with learning problems. Mary became one of his earliest students and the program helped her greatly in her schoolwork. When Vito died suddenly in 1977, it was a very hard time for Mary, now a few months shy of 15. It was also difficult for the rest of the family, as he had always been a devoted father. Mary now looked to her older brothers, Gerry and Lawrence, for the male influence and guidance she no longer had.

Typical of many mothers and daughters, Mary and I experienced some disagreements during those difficult teen-age years. On a homemade Valentine card, in 1980, she wrote:

"Mom, Hope you had a good day. Thanks for dinner and everything else you do for me. I know I can get pretty cranky sometimes but I still love you. Love, Mary."

A mother could not ask for more.

Grandma Peg and Grandpa Jack Malone enjoy a sunny day in the Catskills, New York, 1951.

Grandma Tess (Teresa) Gioia in her apartment in Queens, New York, 1966.

A backyard swing kept Baby Mary happy, 1963.

Birthday sisters, Christine and Mary, enjoy a birthday together, 1964.

Lawrence and Mary at family dining room table, 1966.

Big brother Patrick, and Big Sister Mary try to keep little Danny happy, 1967.

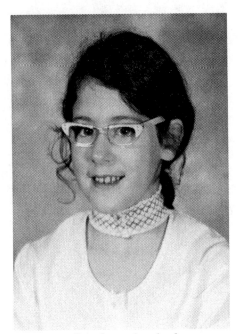

Mary smiles for school photographer, 1968.

Playing with a Yo-Yo on the front steps of 4 Cornelius, 1970.

Hail, hail, the gang's all here and dressed in their Sunday best. Left to right: Gerry, Patrick, Lawrence, Christine (holding on to Mary), Joan and Robert (holding on to Dan) 1967.

Mary and Dan with their father, Vito Gioia, 1976.

The three sisters, Christine, Mary and Joan, pose with proud mother on Joan's wedding day, August 2, 1980.

Mary and Joan are smiling bridesmaids for sister, Christine, October 30, 1982.

Mary and Gato, the family's cherished pet, on the back porch, 1982.

Posing at Patrick's graduation from SUNY Brockport. Left to right: Brenda, Rob's girlfriend; the proud mother, and Mary, May 13, 1984.

Mary and ten-month old Amanda Celentano, the only niece (or nephew) Mary would know, Christmas 1983.

The last time the family was all together. Family photo at brother Gerry and Margie's wedding in Maryland. Left to right: Jeffrey Joyce and Christine; Mike Celentano and Joan; Lawrence and Mary Ann; Mary; Margie and Gerry; mother Pat and Moises; brothers Patrick, Daniel and Robert, May 25, 1985.

One of Mary's many Gingerbread Houses.

Mary's five brothers pose after Laura Elizabeth's baptism, the day after the University of Rochester v. Union College football game. Left to right: Daniel, Patrick, Robert, Gerard and Lawrence, September 20, 1987.

A family portrait at Christine's birthday celebration. Left to right: Back row - Patrick; mother, Pat; Robert; Gerard. Front row - Lawrence, Joan, Christine and Daniel, December 2004.

Mary's Tyrolean boots that march in support of anti-gun violence legislation, 1996.

Joan displays the plaque to be placed at the Berkeley marina near the site of the murders, 1995.

The plaque for Mary and Greg cemented in place at the Cesar E. Chavez Park across from the City of Berkeley. Pictured is one of the trees that sadly did not survive, 1996.

Dan at Van Saun Park, Bergen County, New Jersey, as he dedicated our brick in Mary's name at the Shelter Our Sisters' Pathway to Self Sufficiency, 2003.

Other bricks in memory of Mary. Top to bottom: In the first walkway at the New York State Crime Victims' Memorial in Albany, New York, 1997; at the Albany Hudson River Way, 2001; and at the Journey Home End-of-Life Hospice in Rochester, 2000.

The New York State Crime Victims' Memorial behind the Legislative Office Building in Albany, New York, 2006.

Patrick and wife, Elizabeth, perform at a Crime Victims'
Rights Week Vigil at First Church, Albany, 1994. Patrick
has performed at the Vigil in remembrance of his sister
every year since 1989.

The POMC photo board at National Day of
Remembrance for Murder Victims at Schenectady's
Central Park Rose Garden, September 25, 2000.

Mary Regina Gioia

10

MARY REGINA – PART TWO

In January 1981, Mary completed her high school courses. She had a few months before beginning college. Her interest in food services peaked with her BOCES classes so she investigated several schools offering culinary arts. She chose the Culinary Arts program at Schenectady County Community College (SCCC). Her choice was made for several reasons—the cost, and she was interested in a young man who lived in the Albany area. Mary met Mark at BOCES; it was her first serious relationship.

She continued waitressing at the neighborhood Friendly's Restaurant and living at home. In March, she approached me with a plan. "Ma, I found a better job as a waitress at the Vineyard Restaurant on Western Avenue in Albany. Since I don't have the money to buy a car yet, Mark's parents offered me a room in their home so I can be near work. What do you think?"

Surprised, but willing to listen, I said: "Mary, I don't know if that's a good idea. Let me think about it." I knew I was being cautious. After all, she was only eighteen years old. I felt I needed to think about it.

Not to be put off easily, she urged, "But, Ma, I have a better job over in Albany. Please. I need to do this."

In the back of my mind, I could hear, *Parents need to know when to be firm and when to compromise.* Mary never gave me any trouble; maybe I should bend a little. So, reluctantly I said, "Okay, but I want to meet Mark's parents and talk this over with them."

Mary and I drove over to Mark's house one night after work. We were both a bit anxious. Their house was a modest one, located near the beginning of the Northway, and true to what Mary had told me, close to Western Avenue. I met Mark's parents. They were quite cordial and appeared to genuinely like Mary. They showed me the room Mary would have, and they appeared quite comfortable with the arrangement. Still slightly hesitant, I finally agreed to have her try it out. On the ride home, we were both rather quiet. I think we recognized this would be her first real break from the family.

In June, Mary graduated with her class from Niskayuna High School. She continued to live at Mark's in Albany, now also working as a chambermaid at the Ramada Inn, near the Vineyard.

Some years later, I had an uncanny experience. I regularly had my hair cut at a salon on Western Avenue. When my hairdresser, a young woman named Tanya left to have a baby, she referred me to her co-worker, Joe. My first appointment with him was memorable. He saw me many times with Tanya at the salon so he was quite cordial. But as he cut my hair, I could see his image behind me in the mirror. He seemed nervous.Suddenly, he stopped, scissors in mid-air, and burst out, "I used to cut your daughter Mary's hair."

Turning to him, with a smile, I said, "Oh, really, when was that?"

"She would come in here with her friend, Mark, and a few times I trimmed her hair too. I was afraid to say anything. I thought it would upset you."

I assured him that I was always happy to hear anyone tell me they had known my daughter. Hearing her name gives life to her again, even if only for a moment.

Then, with a grin, I said, "Well, Mary's beautiful thick and curly dark hair is certainly a contrast to mine!" Since that day, a special bond exists between Joe and me.

In the fall of 1981, Mary returned to Schenectady to begin classes at SCCC. Although she and Moises got along fairly well, a degree of tension loomed when she was home. Her free spirit and his more somber ways often did not mix. Well aware of this and not wanting to cause problems for me, she asked to stay with my friends, Doris and Bill Aiken. They had a large home close to SCCC, which helped Mary who did not own a car. Their house, three stories high, had innumerable rooms and for many years was a residence for Ellis Hospital's student doctors. There, Mary had her own space on the third floor, and could come and go between classes and meeting with friends.

Mary threw herself into her courses at SCCC, thriving there, learning what most interested her. Matteo A. Casola, one of her instructors, and an icon for the college foods program, said

> *I had Mary in Food Administration and Menu Plan and Organization and Management 1 and 2. I also taught her in a Labor Relations class. She was well liked by everybody .One thing I remember is that she never hesitated to volunteer for any project we had. One time, as part of a Dining Room class, her assignment was to manage a special affair for the College's Board of Trustees. Many of the important people supporting the College were at it. The owner of Jack's Restaurant in Albany and Marvin from the Van Dyke (two prestigious establishments at the time) were there. Mary had to make up the menu, and she handled it very nicely.*

It's so good to hear comments like this, as Mary was never one to boast or brag. Before the event, she came to me with a request. "Ma, can I borrow those dressy black pants of yours? Mine are too casual. There's this event at school and I have to look a bit more formal." When she donned her white shirt and those black pants, she looked quite dapper, in charge. I wish I could have been there to see her in action.

When Casola mentioned the Labor Relations course, I recalled Mary had a peaked interest in this class. She seemed adamant about union representation for food workers. I wonder if her strong conviction sprang from our family's solid support of Cesar Chavez in the '60s for his efforts to unionize lettuce workers in California. She no doubt remembered that we would not buy lettuce from the supermarket unless it had a union label.

Mary became a member of a local union representing commercial food workers when she worked for the Freihofer

Baking Company. As a Baker's Assistant there from June of 1982 to January 1983, she was very happy when she originally got this job. Freihofer's was a well-known commodity in our house. Our next-door neighbor, Faye Foster, worked many years for Freihofer's and had one of the last horse-drawn routes in Schenectady. Not to mention that for many years, our home freezer overflowed with half-priced day-old baked goods from the Freihofer plant on Albany Street.

But Mary was somewhat disappointed when her main duty at Freihofer's was to "assist in large-scale production of bread" (from her resume). She described it to me this way, "It actually means, Mom, that I put the pans of bread into the oven and retrieve them when done." And again from her resume, "Observed breads for quality control." Granted her tasks may not have been in line with her skills, but I assured her she was learning something important - to work with others to produce a product. And her resume also stated that at SCCC, she assisted in the production of the World's Longest Loaf of Bread. There must have been a good deal of collaboration on that project!

Mary recognized that if she were to be more independent, she needed her own car. Seeing an ad for a 1977 Plymouth Volare, she asked her brother, Lawr, to look at it with her, along with Joan who helped her learn to drive. After Lawr tested it and it seemed in good condition, Mary now had her own wheels. More job possibilities opened up such as the one at Carasello's Bakery in downtown Albany. There she did some baking, preparing rolls for the oven. Working the counter at that Italian bakery, with her dark curly hair and hazel eyes, she was often mistaken for a member of the Carasello family.

Mary was excited when the first Bruegger's Bagel shop came to the Capital District. She called me saying, "Mom, I was hired and will help set up the store at Stuyvesant Plaza. At last, I'll work in a real bakery." Here, too, she was not assigned to baking; instead, she was in charge of making the daily soups. She became quite proficient at this, and, having tasted many of her flavorful broths, I can attest to it. Still today, I cannot pass a Bruegger's store without having many memories of Mary's happiness in working at one.

Mary was always in the midst of our family events. She was a bridesmaid at Joan's wedding in August 1980. And when

Lawrence and Mary Ann were married in August 1982, Mary helped with all the food preparation for the Rehearsal Dinner held at our house. How I appreciated that.

Her birthday sister, Christine, was married in October 1982. Mary and Joan were bridesmaids. When I glance at a photo of that beautiful day I keep on my bureau, it reveals three sisters smiling, their happiness bubbling over. A garland of white roses and baby breath cascades down Chris' blonde hair; Mary and Joan each have a pink rose tucked in their dark brown locks. Chris, holding a bouquet of white roses, wears a white lace, dancer-length dress, with puffed sleeves. White ballet slippers complete her ensemble. Joan, six months pregnant, wears a long-sleeve turquoise-blue, below-the-knee dress. And Mary, ever casual, wears a gray, short-sleeved blouse, dotted with small pink flowers, and a plum-colored, below-the-knee full skirt. Mary and Joan hold single pink rose bouquets.

A bridal shower for Chris was held at our house. Working full-time, I gladly relinquished the food planning and preparation responsibilities to Mary. She was happy to be able to put her talents to the test. A tray of hors d'oeuvres tickled our appetites for her main course of carrot soup, cold cuts, salad, and delicious crusty bread. When I asked her how she did all of this, she looked at me, smugly, and said, "Well, Ma, what do you think I've been doing at school?" And she was right; she was learning well.

Mary met John at SCCC. By the end of 1982, they were a couple. One of her teachers told me, "They were the cutest couple. When you saw one, you saw the other. They were always together." They had many mutual friends from school and there were always gatherings, parties and concerts to attend.

Mary and John both worked at Lake George during her last two summers. Mary loved Lake George, with the scenic Adirondack Mountains surrounding it. She was a chambermaid in one of the small motels on the Lake, and several notes of appreciation she kept revealed the personal service she gave her customers. For Mary, it was almost like being on vacation, with a little work thrown in. A small job at a craft shop in town enriched her artistic skills.

When Mary left for California, she left a box filled with colorful stringed beads at home. She had used one long strand as a room divider in an apartment. Now, I often string a strand of these colorful beads on my Christmas trees, where, with the tree lights lit, her beads still glow and sparkle. I also put a string of these beads around her grave stone.

Mary and John kept up their close relationship until the summer of 1984, when, as with many young people, problems arose. But their friendship continued. In Mary's last letter, she mentions him.

"You can now see what one of my crazy letters is like! I write them all the time to my friends! I wrote John a 20 page goofy letter written on everything from paper resembling tie-dye shirts…."

Both John and Mark were at Mary's memorial service and her burial.

When Mary returned to Schenectady in the fall of 1984, her siblings living in Boston begged her to consider relocating there. Chris lived and worked there for several years. Later, Robert and Patrick followed. With all the good restaurants in that city, they tried to entice Mary to move to the Massachusetts capital. But Mary, with a preference for a slower pace, decided against it.

Mary, Dan and I drove over to explore Boston one weekend and had a good time with the family there. A fast visit to Filene's Basement (the genuine one), saw us tearing around, intent on finding bargains. I bought a colorful, peasant-style skirt for myself but soon realized it was perfect for Mary and relinquished it to her. A highlight of the trip was our boat tour of Boston Harbor. Many years later, Chris sent me a photo she took of Mary and me on that day. It prompted me to write:

A happy day on Boston Harbor,
When our spirits soared high.
Blue sky, no rain in sight to darken the horizon
Hair dancing in the warm ocean breeze,
N'ere a sweater-wearing day as we toured the City's sights.
Her leather strap bracelet matching her handbag strap
Both gracing strong tanned arms.

On the ride home to Schenectady, we stopped at every shoe store along the Massachusetts Turnpike. Mary wanted a new pair of Birkenstocks; nothing else would do. At the time, I had never heard of Birkenstocks and wondered why she couldn't settle for any of the other sandals in the stores. Now I own a pair, which I purchased on one of Mary's anniversaries. Wearing them brings me closer to her. And Mary was right—they are very comfortable.

During that last fall of 1984, Mary worked for a software company in Ballston Lake before leaving for Vermont in December. When they learned of Mary's death, I received a letter from the Manager:

> *Mary was not here in our employ for a long time but we all remember her fondly. She was charming, bubbly and always did her tasks in a superior manner. I truly enjoyed having her on my staff. I am enclosing a postcard which Mary sent us shortly after she arrived in Vermont. I had it hanging on the wall in my office with other postcards of New England. I thought you might like it for a souvenir.*

The card showed a beautiful winter scene in a quaint New England village—just what Mary loved. On it, she wrote:

> *Here's another pretty postcard for your collection…Things are going really good up here. These Vermonters are wonderful. I found a little cabin in Moretown, VT to live in. It's really neat…Well hope you all have a wonderful Christmas and a great year ahead. You will!*
>
> *Lots of love to you all, Mary (with her signature rose she often added to her name).*

In Vermont, Mary held down two jobs from the end of 1984 into the spring of 1985. At the Sugarbush ski area, she worked in food preparation, and she was a waitress at China Barn. Joan recalls sending Mary's Christmas gifts that year with her brother-in-law, Dave, who went on a ski trip to Sugarbush. I mailed her mine—a long, winter-weight nightgown and woolen gloves, necessities for the cold mountains of Vermont. Mary's

Christmas gift to the family that year was delicious homemade chocolate candies, decorated as only Mary could do.

As a young girl, and then into womanhood, Mary was very much aware of our family's political views, appearing to mirror them. She too had certain causes she was passionate about. Her final letter mentioned the Hiroshima bombing, irradiated food, Nicaragua. At home, she left a folder she titled, "Important Files." Within it were several newsletters from the Honest Weight Food Co-Op in Albany, the one she wanted to alert about food irradiation, and a card to be addressed to a Member of Congress about "Shifting the Burden" from tax giveaways and military buildup to programs for people.

In 1983, I attended a protest at the Seneca Falls Army Depot. Our mission was to protest the possible storage of nuclear weapons at the Depot. Mary asked to ride along on the bus with other women and me from Schenectady. It was a 2 1/2 hour bus ride on the Thruway to the Depot. Once there, we joined scores of other women activists from all over the northeast. I was proud that she asked to come and that she mingled so easily with the other women. A friend, Gladys, who was also there, wrote to me when she heard of Mary's murder:

> I remember Mary so well on the Seneca Falls trip – a pretty, sweet, concerned young person – and how good it was to have concerned young people as participants for good causes. I remember her too, when she came to the library for some help with her resume—and remember your talking about her hopes to be recognized as a professional baker – and now she is gone.

Another memory regarding Mary's political views was the Presidential Election of 1984. I was at home alone, watching the returns. Mary stopped in for a while to join me and sat on the floor in front of the television. She became upset as the final numbers trickled in for the Mondale-Ferraro ticket.

"I can't believe it, Mom, what's happening? Geraldine Ferraro would be a great Vice-President."

I thought of this a few years later when, on a return trip from Rochester, I stopped at Seneca Falls, where I visited the

National Women's Hall of Fame. Yes, Mary, there, listed with all the other great women, was Geraldine Ferraro.

Her last birthday card to me, in February '85, was a classic. The front of the card has peasant-looking farmers tending to their vegetables and sunflowers. "Happy Birthday" is spelled out with large green letters on manicured bushes. Inside the card, the message reads:

> *There once was a gardener conservative*
> *Who used neither spray nor preservative*
> *I asked him to do*
> *Something special for you,*
> *And I hope you agree, it's superlative!*
> *Have a Great Birthday and a Super Year!*
>   *(s) Love you lots, Mary*

Next to the line describing the gardener, she inserted, "must have been a Democrat!".

Mary continued to work in Vermont until the beginning of May 1985. When she returned to Schenectady, she asked Joan if she could live with her for a short time. She contemplated a trip out west, but since her brother, Gerry, was to be married on May 25th, she needed to stay in the area until then. Never without working, she picked up an interim job, working for a local house cleaning service for a few weeks.

Joan and Mike drove Mary and Dan to Maryland for Gerry and Margie's wedding. All of Mary's sisters and brothers were in the wedding party. Mary had such a good time. I can still see her dancing up a storm with one of Margie's cousins. At the wedding, she talked about her plans to go out west to Colorado where she had friends. We didn't know it at the time, but this would be the last time she was with all of the family.

Mary lived at Joan's during the month of June. Joan's birthday was June 20th. Mary awoke early that morning and sneaked down to the kitchen to begin baking a cake for Joan. Mike, Joan's husband, was awakened, hearing a strange sound, like someone scratching on something. When he wandered out to the kitchen, there was Mary scraping the many carrots for the carrot cake. After breakfast, Joan dropped her off at the bus terminal. Mary was on her way to Wisconsin to a Grateful Dead concert.

A week later, she returned to Schenectady to attend the Dead concert at the Saratoga Performing Arts Center (SPAC). Joan remembered Mary arrived home early in the morning the day after that concert—it was Friday, June 28th. Joan wrote in her journal:

> *She knocked on the back door and came in and said she had to get some clothes because she was going to go to some other Dead shows—also, she had to get her things from a Dead-on bus that had broken down in Ohio. We went in the bathroom and talked for a few minutes while she washed up a little....Then she left, I remember standing on the front porch watching the car pull away that she was in...*

That was the last time Joan saw her little sister alive.

Mary called Joan on July 4th from Illinois. She was getting a ride to California. Joan heard from her four times that month from California, one time at 12:30am. Mary forgot about the time differential! They spoke again just before Joan went on vacation. A decision had to be made on what to do with Samson, her cat. Mary said she would call when Joan was back from vacation. They never spoke again.

11

A WEEK LATER

We survived the hardest week of our lives. Now we had to move on - without Mary. As we tried to deal with her death, Moises increasingly isolated himself from us. He didn't know how to act or react. Nor did we, but as a family we attempted to stay focused on what had to be done. Relations between Moises and me were already strained, and our few sessions with a marriage counselor had not helped. Perhaps it was too difficult for us to change our ways—or our families—at this point in our lives. Several incidents confirmed for me that our life together was over.

On the night before Mary's Memorial, many of Gerry and Lawr's friends arrived from Connecticut, from Boston, from all over, to be there for them. They congregated in the backyard at the picnic table, having a few beers, talking, trying to lift their spirits. It seemed almost normal to hear animated talk and laughter again at the house.

I sat in the living room talking with my brother, Marty, who had just arrived from Miami. Moises called me from the upstairs bedroom. He sounded quite agitated. He had gone to bed without saying goodnight. I called up to him and asked what was wrong.

"I'm very tired. You know, Pat, I haven't had much sleep the last few nights.If that party out in the yard doesn't break up right away, I'm going to call the Niskayuna police."

Those words sent shock waves through my body. I quickly told him, "The Niskayuna Police were here three nights ago, and if I can help it, they won't come through my door again."

When I sat down, I was shaking so much, Marty noticed it immediately. Gerry and Lawr spoke to their friends and they soon left.

The tension continued. After the Memorial service on Tuesday, Moises' strange behavior and isolation from us became more noticeable. My brother and some of my close friends were now also aware of it. I told them I was struggling with a difficult decision. Would I continue to try to keep Moises happy, which was proving to be almost impossible, or would I again take charge of my own life? At the end of that day, the answer was clearer.

Later that week, I confronted Moises and told him I wanted a separation. He became extremely upset and tried to dissuade me. He promised he would change, but my mind was made up. Nothing, no one, would ever come between my family and me again. I learned later many marriages fall apart when a family member is murdered or dies unexpectedly. Our relationship had already been damaged for many other reasons. But Mary's death was the final blow.

A few days after Mary's burial, amid much arguing and pleading from Moises, I moved out of my house temporarily, taking only a few changes of clothing and toiletries with me. I moved in with my friends, Doris and Bill Aiken. Eerily, I now occupied the same space on the third floor of the Aiken's large home that Mary had when she stayed there. I had to prove to Moises that I was deadly serious about the separation. He remained stubborn and refused to leave the house. I stayed at the Aiken's until November, when Moises finally moved out of the house and took an apartment with a friend until he could find better living arrangements.

Once he moved out and agreed to the separation, we were able to be "friends" for a number of years. But our relationship was never the same. After he retired from his job with the State, he became nervous that I might hedge in on his pension benefits. When I opted to not seek any part of his pension, he then agreed to a divorce, which became final in August 1990. Moises died on November 29, 1993. Joan and I attended his wake, and I went to his funeral mass and burial.

At the time of the trial, Moises wrote to the Judge. Although he and I had our own difficulties, the sentiments he expressed revealed that he loved Mary in his own way.

> My name is Dr. Moises Riano and I was
> Mary's stepfather. I knew her since she was a child
> and I was quite fond of her. She was bright and
> ambitious...but, at the same time, she was rather
> innocent and trusted people. She could not stand
> violence and was always praying for peace.
> Unfortunately, her life was too short to see her goals
> achieved.
>
> This case causes me to believe that life is
> very ironic. I have been dedicated for many years to
> cancer research, trying to apply my knowledge in
> an effort to mitigate human suffering. This requires
> countless hours of work and dedication, but if at the
> end we can save a human life from illness or pro-
> long life span for some years, this itself is a reward.
> On the other hand, how easy it is for somebody who
> does not value life to destroy it in its best years.
> Probably, this is part of life, but it is rather difficult
> for somebody like me, or for most people, to accept
> such a philosophy.

After Mary's burial, most of the family returned to their homes. Gerry and Lawr stayed on to attend their boyhood friend, Gene Leary's wedding. Margie drove to New Jersey alone to attend her brother's wedding. I was invited to Gene's wedding too, as I had a long relationship with the Leary family from earlier days in the Christian Family Movement. Although at first reluctant, my family persuaded me to go. Everyone felt it might help to raise my spirits. One of the hardest things to face is that life does go on. We either join it or stay locked in our own despair.

The marriage ceremony took place at St. John the Evangelist Church. I arrived early and sat in the pew awaiting the start of the service. This beautiful church could well match any European cathedral. I gazed at the artistic and ornate statues of angels, the four evangelists, and myriad saints spread around its interior. They appeared to call to me to revitalize my faith in God. As I sat there, my mind wandered to other happier times in that church, when Joan and Mike were married, and Mary and Christine and my other children were in the wedding party. Amanda was baptized there too. I have a photo of Mary, the proud aunt, sitting in the pew behind the proud parents. It was not easy to put aside my own grief and sadness, but being with so many faithful and kind friends helped me to appear normal for a time. At the reception, I sat at a table with friends, who quickly drew me into their spirited conversations. At the end of the evening, even I was amazed that I was able to smile and be part of the world again if only briefly.

The next day, Sunday, we drove Dan back to the University of Rochester (U of R). He had to get back for football practice as he was on the team. Joan, Mike, and Lawr, who took time off from a summer internship with Polychrome in Yonkers, accompanied me. They knew Dan needed support at this time. He remained quite despondent over Mary's death. He even spoke about not going back to school. I asked him, as only a mother could, "So, what are you going to do? Hang around here with me?" I said it with a smile but meant every word. "Mary would want you, her little brother, to go back and lead those Yellow Jackets (his football team) to victory."

Recently, I spoke to Dan about what was going on with him at that time.

> You go from not believing it, and then shocked into asking how does this all fit into the grand scheme of life? Is it worth going back to school, to continue to lead your daily life? What is it all worth? If something as terrible, as horrible as this can happen, I didn't feel like going back to my life as it was before.

But he did go back, hard as that was for him.

We pulled up to the U of R campus after our three-hour ride. Some of Dan's fraternity brothers, including his "big brother" Sam Guerrieri, spotted him right away. With their arms around his shoulder, they walked him back to his dorm. When I saw this, I knew Dan would be okay. Before we left, we met with Dan's two football coaches, Coach Tellier and Coach Vitone.

They were extremely kind and assured us they would keep an eye on Dan. Coach Vitone, the older of the two, whispered in my ear, "Don't worry about Dan, we'll take care of him." Somehow I believed that this tough, tenacious, father figure would do just as he promised.

That next week I was back at my job in the State Senate. During off-Session months at the Legislature, I worked alone in the Albany office; the rest of the Senator's staff was in Manhattan. It felt as if I was emerging from a cocoon. Last week, we had concentrated so intently on what needed to be done that my head was still spinning. Perhaps it would take some time for reality to set in but this was a start.

Everyone I met at work had heard about Mary's murder. Co-workers from other offices filed in, one by one, expressing condolences and offering any help they could give. It was important to let other people express their sadness too. As I received my co-workers' hugs, I began to feel alive and an active participant in life.

I found that some of my attitudes and demeanor had changed when dealing with the public. When constituents called the office for help with problems, it was hard to put things into perspective. I would listen to them, many times wanting to shout, *You consider this a problem? Suppose your daughter had been brutally murdered?* Needless to say, I kept these pervasive thoughts hidden and did what I needed to do to solve their issues.

When I was back in my office, I had a vague remembrance of a letter addressed to the Senator from a homicide support group. At the time, I was struck by its stark name and brought it to the Senator's attention. As a father of two children, he was shocked that a group such as this even existed. Now I became determined to find it. From my experience with Remove Intoxicated Drivers (RID), I knew survivors of a crime, or family members, could receive support from others who had experienced a similar situation. I contacted a young woman on the Senate staff and asked if she could help me find them. Within a few days, I had the name.

Parents Of Murdered Children (POMC), an organization no one *wants* to join. I phoned Robin Stambler, the leader and founder of the local Albany chapter. We spoke at some length and I told her what had happened to Mary. Robin was very compassionate and supportive as she told me about the group and where they held meetings.

Joan and I attended our first POMC meeting that September. We were nervous as we entered the meeting room, but immediately received a sympathetic and warm welcome. Their many hugs felt genuine. They had been where we were now. We heard members tell their stories about the loss of loved ones and recount their experience with the criminal justice system, some good, some bad. Seeing some members smiling, even laughing, I thought, "I hope we'll be able to be like that someday too." That first meeting, in September 1985, commenced my long association with Parents Of Murdered Children and Other Survivors of Homicide Victims.

I knew I had to make another telephone call. This one would be difficult. Early that September, I contacted Greg's dad, David Kniffin. He lived in Wilton, Connecticut. We talked a long while on the phone, already feeling the bond between our two families. Greg was David's only son; he also had a daughter. He and Greg's mother were divorced. David and I would get to know each other very well over the next months on the telephone, and later when we attended the trial the following May.

12

THE NEXT FEW WEEKS

In the weeks that followed, the California police and the district attorney's office in Alameda County stayed in contact with me. I received more information on what happened to Mary, and updates on the case. On September 5th, Assistant District Attorney Jeff Horner called to say that Ralph Thomas, the prime suspect, had been arraigned on two counts of first-degree murder and special circumstances. I asked what that meant.

"It means Thomas is alleged to have killed two people." Thomas was the man in the crowd at the waterfront who said he thought it was Mary as her body was being recovered from the water.

I shuddered as Horner told me more about Thomas' background, realizing that Mary was with him that night. But who wears their rap sheet on their sleeve? Thomas served nine years in San Quentin Prison previously for committing 13 felonies in Alameda County and a neighboring County in 1974. Horner continued,

It will be based on circumstantial evidence. No eyewitness who saw Thomas kill Mary and Greg has come forward but evidence against him appears strong. The police found shell casings in his car that were the same as those used to murder Mary and Greg, and Thomas claims his gun was stolen during the night. The police also questioned him about how he was able to identify the body as Mary's when she was some distance away in the water, and he didn't know her very well.

As I tried to absorb what Horner said, I asked, "Okay, what's next?"

A Preliminary Hearing will be held in the Berkeley Municipal Court on September 18th. Thomas will plead not guilty. If the Judge determines there is enough evidence of guilt, the case will move on to the Alameda County Superior Court. There, it could be heard by a Judge, with Thomas' defense waiving a jury. But the District Attorney could insist on a jury. Either way, it won't go to trial until early next year and will probably last a month, or longer. The District Attorney will seek the death penalty and there will be sequestered voir dire.

"What's that?" I asked. Like most victim survivors, I was getting lost in legal jargon.

Horner realized it was becoming technical so he quickly replied, "That means each juror will be interviewed individually. It could take a long time until a proper jury is found."

"Is it possible to find anyone in the area who would not know Thomas' background?"

"Good point. We'll try our best to find jurors who at least indicate they will put that out of their minds during the trial."

Then I asked Horner what he thought about the media coverage thus far. He said he thought they were insensitive, almost downright mean about our family privacy, especially the way the picture of Mary had been painted. But he felt the media had done no irrevocable harm up to now.

About the circumstantial evidence in the case, he said, "Yes, that's all we have."

"What about that woman who says Ralph Thomas didn't do it?"

"We believe she was Ralph's girlfriend. Of course, her bias would be to exonerate him."

Horner gave me some good news when he told me that

Inspector Wolke, a key investigator in our case, was one of the best detectives in Berkeley—very experienced, very compassionate. He then promised to call my boss, Senator Franz Leichter, who was an attorney. Franz had some legal questions and I needed all the help I could get to sort everything out. California was, in my mind, a world away.

Jeff Horner was my initial contact with the District Attorney's office, but Assistant District Attorney Jim Anderson would prosecute the case. He was an experienced and skillful prosecutor. A fast talker, who minced no words, he had already handled numerous death penalty cases. (A while back, Jim, now retired, was quoted in the press about the Laci Peterson case in California. Her husband, Scott Peterson, was convicted based on circumstantial evidence for murdering Laci and her unborn fetus. Several grisly similarities to our case stood out. Laci was found in San Francisco Bay; Mary and Greg were also discovered in a section of the Bay. Our case was also based on circumstantial evidence. Anderson, who had put ten men on death row, stated that it was now more difficult for even seasoned homicide prosecutors to win over jurors to render the death penalty in the second trial, the penalty phase.)

During my first telephone conversation with Jim, he described the scenario the defense would likely use in the case. A woman, who lived in her car with her two children at Rainbow Village, said she saw a blonde-haired man follow Mary and Greg. She claimed they argued. The man had something in his hand—a big stick, maybe a gun. She said she saw him later wiping blood, or something, from his hands on the ground.

As Jim gave me his theory about this story, it was typical of his blunt style. He began, "Harry and his ugly little bitch, Vivian," and conjectured that she told this tale, prompted by Harry Shorman, her boyfriend, one of the founders of Rainbow Village. If she became a material witness, she would be housed and protected by Alameda County, perhaps at the nearby motel on the Marina, far better digs than living out of her car. Jim told me he contacted the Bureau of Marine & Fisheries to get the oceanographic report for that night, which revealed there was no moon; instead, it was overcast and foggy. He concluded the story was totally contrived. How could she have seen all she said she saw? Many more conversations with Jim Anderson would follow in the weeks ahead.

I continued to stay at the Aiken's home for the first few months after Mary's murder. Doris and I were good friends. We worked together on numerous political campaigns, including her unsuccessful run for an Assembly seat. Doris, through RID, helped many victims of drunk drivers and their families write their victim impact statements to be read before the court. Now she wrote one to tell the Judge in our case about the impact of Mary's murder.

> You may regard this letter as a victim's impact statement, as I am part of a much larger community severely damaged by the untimely and cruel death of Mary Gioia. Having a long and close relationship with the Gioia family, Mary chose to live with us for a while.
> We felt lucky to have the opportunity to have Mary among us. She fit in immediately, and never complained even though she had to share all amenities with my very disorganized and eccentric son afflicted with manic depression.
> Mary was a warm, hardworking, cheerful young person, talented in the domestic arts and eager to share her talents with everyone. Her interests were peace in her time, music and making the place she was in, wherever that was, a congenial, comfortable, and friendly scene.
> WHOEVER KILLED HER SO WANTONLY, MUST NEVER BE ALLOWED TO BE AMONG CIVILIZED PEOPLE AGAIN. This is the only comfort that you can give the family and friends of Mary. It isn't much, but it is all the criminal justice system can offer.

During those first few weeks, the Aikens provided the encouragement and support I needed to sort through my current predicament. The shock of Mary's murder, coupled with a desperate feeling that I had to remain strong for my family when our world was crumbling, had finally brought me to take this step, to separate from Moises. Other considerations swirled around in my mind. My marriage to Vito, the children's father, had ended in divorce so I was extremely hesitant to go through another. What kind of an example was this for my family? Is divorce always the answer when things go awry? On the other hand, I knew my family was behind me in this decision.

Those first weeks were particularly hard too for others in the family. In her journal, Joan wrote:

> *Monday, September 2, 1:00am. Just talked to Chris on the phone for a little while. She is in Burnt Hills this weekend for a wedding. I got upset a little while ago—looking over some of Mary's recipes—started crying—just wanted to talk to someone special— like my sister, Chris. Because only she and I have the exact same feeling of loss over our little sister. It's different for everyone, but for Chris and me, I think it is the same, and it is such a comfort to know I have Chris, and always will. As I always will have Mary also. What a hard and tragic and depressing time of my life this is. Don't really know how to deal or cope with it. Just to keep in real close touch with my family is helping. And to keep in touch with my friends and Mary's friends also. I'm so glad I have her address book!*

Other decisions were needed. Less than two weeks after Mary's death, Joan and I met with the Board of Directors of the Schenectady Arts Council. They called to discuss the memorial bequests they were receiving. Their office was located on the second floor above Proctor's Theatre in downtown Schenectady. To reach it, we walked through the tiny mall-like area where the Carl Company department store had been. Memories of the many times I had brought the children down to see a movie at Proctor's or to shop at Carl's—happier days—danced across my mind.

As Joan and I entered the Council room, a hush came upon the group. What do you say to a mother and sister of a murdered victim? Looking around the room, I quickly recognized

Kay Ackerman. She and her husband, Don, had been friends for many years. Suddenly, I felt more comfortable. At least I knew one member of the Board.

Joan and I were introduced. I took a deep breath and spoke briefly about what had happened to Mary and why our family chose the Arts Council as recipient of her memorial contributions.

"I suppose it was because Mary really enjoyed working with her hands. She loved sketching. She filled drawing pads after drawing pads with flowers, especially roses, cartoon characters, cats and anything else that she thought about at the time. We felt she had talent but, sadly, didn't have enough time to explore it. And she loved music, all kinds. One of my family suggested the Arts Council and it just seemed right to all of us."

It may have been one of the first times the Council had been chosen to receive memorial funds; they seemed uncertain how to use the money. They assured us that they would consider a number of avenues, including a possible scholarship. Meanwhile, incoming funds would be put into an escrow account and the names of contributors sent to us. On the way home, Joan and I realized that we had just spoken about Mary's murder to a group of strangers, albeit sympathetic ones, and we had had the strength to do so.

By the beginning of November, I moved back to our family home as Moises had finally moved to an apartment with a friend. The first day I walked into 4 Cornelius Avenue, a feeling of emptiness overwhelmed me. A vacuum existed, a gap that begged to be filled. Mary hadn't lived home for several years but many of her things remained upstairs in the third floor bedroom, the one that she had last used. Joan and I started looking through them but were quickly overcome with sadness. Each piece of clothing or jewelry we picked up, each book or piece of paper with her scribbles, depressed us. We decided to wait until other family members were home to dispose of her belongings. That would give everyone a chance to choose something to remember her by.

About that time, Doris, always looking out for her friend, invited me to accompany her for a weekend at the Kripalu Center in Lenox, Massachusetts. Her two daughters, Jane and Mary Gale, lived in the community formed there. Doris and her close friend, Eva, thought it might help me to get away for a few days, to someplace new. Kripalu was well known for its yoga and other programs designed to help people find peace in their lives. Exactly what I needed.

Kripalu is located on the site of a former Jesuit seminary, an idyllic and tranquil setting on several acres of green rolling hills, in western Massachusetts. It maintained a strict regimen with a macrobiotic diet, definitely different from my usual fare. Although most of it tasted good, it would take a while to become accustomed to it, especially the serving of only herb teas and no coffee. Strict silence was maintained at mealtimes, difficult to do while seated across from Doris and Eva. It reminded me of Catholic retreats I attended years ago. All of this might not have contributed to relaxation and healing for me, but the cama-raderie with Eva and Doris during that time made up for it. In fact, we had some light moments. After a day without caffeine, we snuck into Jane's room where she was illegally brewing some delicious latte for the three strung-out weekenders. It tasted even better knowing that we had become "coffee convicts."

While I participated in a number of the scheduled activ-ities, it was not easy to let go of many sad feelings; visions of Mary popped into my mind. On reflection, it may have been because many of the residents at Kripalu, young and idealistic, reminded me very much of my daughter. But, overall, this "Stress-Free Weekend" lived up to its name.

With Dan away at the University of Rochester, the fami-ly tried to attend as many of his football games as possible to sup-port him. The rest of us had husbands, wives, each other to talk to. He was by himself, away at college. At least we could give this rough and tough guy a hug after a game and stay connected.

As the year was winding down, a difficult day loomed on our family calendar – December 20th – Mary's birthday. She would have been 23 years old. It was also Christine's birthday, and we knew it would be particularly hard for her—the first without her little birthday sister. We held a family meeting over the telephone; it was decided that we would all go to Boston to be with Chris and to be together that day.

December 20th was a Friday. Since it was the start of a weekend it was easier for most of us to get there. Joan and I left from Schenectady in the early afternoon for the three-hour drive on the Massachusetts Turnpike. Lawr drove up from Hartsdale in his yellow Toyota truck after he finished classes at Columbia. Robert and Patrick already lived in Boston. Dan was the only one missing; he had exams at college and couldn't get away.

Gerry and Margie flew in from Maryland, bringing with them a very special bottle of wine for dinner. It had been a gift from Mary in the picnic basket she had made up for their wedding present. Mary had called me when she was putting together the basket. "Mom, what kind of wine should I buy?"

"Red and dry," I told her. And it was.

The dinner was at Rob and Brenda's apartment in Malden. We talked into the wee hours of the morning. We laughed, we cried, we drank the delicious red wine and we knew, oh, yes, we knew, Mary was right there with us. Oh, how she loved family celebrations.

13

THE PRELIMINARY HEARING BEGINS

California still was a world away in my mind. It became closer when I heard from a friend out in Berkeley. Dick Stearns taught at the University of California and would be there until mid-December. He sent me local newspaper articles about the murders and offered to help in any way he could. We would take him up on this when Gerry and I went to California for the preliminary hearing, where a judge would decide if the evidence is sufficient for the case to move to trial.

Jim Anderson called to say the hearing was set for October 30th. I told him, "I'll be there."

"Well, you can come but there's nothing you can do at it," he responded in his usual clipped manner.

"Look, if there's something going on, anywhere, involving one of my kids, I'll be there. If it's postponed—or anything like that, please let me know."

On Tuesday, October 29th, after an early hair appointment, I hopped into my car to begin the 2 1/2 hour trip down the Taconic Parkway to Hartsdale, where Lawr and Mary Ann lived. It was usually an enjoyable trip. But I began to feel anxious as I neared my destination. There would be the six-hour flight to California, and then what? How would I react when I saw the man accused of murdering Mary...murdering my daughter? I now knew his name, Ralph Thomas, and learned about his lengthy criminal background. He was also known as "International" because some people at Rainbow Village had so dubbed him as his birthday was around July 4th. Make sense? No, but nothing did at this point.

When I arrived at Lawr's, we drove to Newark Airport where we met Gerry who flew in from Maryland. Our flight was on People's Express to Oakland. As our case moved forward, I became very familiar with that airline and its reasonable fares.

The trip west felt surreal. I always wanted to see more of the states but had neither the time nor opportunity to do so. But here I am on my way to California. I could move around freely in the large airplane. After a few hours, I got out of my seat and stood near a window and looked down. Were those really the tops of the Rocky Mountains below? Or were they clouds simulating mountains? I thought of Mary and her love of mountains. Had she seen them too on her way to California?

When we arrived at Oakland, we rented a car at the airport. This was my first trip to California. I felt so far away from home, from everyone I loved. I was glad Gerry was with me. I know I could not have done this by myself. We drove over to Berkeley, a city of hills, with houses dotted all along roads leading ever upward. I kept imagining Mary walking along these same sidewalks and streets. How excited she must have been, in a new place, beginning a new life.

We arrived at the home of Dick and Charlotte Stearns, where we spent the night. They did everything possible to make us feel comfortable. I don't recall sleeping more than a few hours. My mind, filled with uncertainties about the next day, wouldn't shut down.

In the morning, we drove to the Berkeley Municipal Court. When I saw the Courthouse, I knew that this was not a dream - this was real. A small group of people congregated outside. One, a slightly disheveled woman, with tousled brown hair, between 25 to 30 years old, quickly made her way over to speak to me. She began, "I'm sorry about Mary. I told her to come in my car if she was afraid but she said no, she'd be okay." I realized then I was standing before the woman who had a radically different picture of what had happened that terrible night. I thanked her and quickly excused myself. I did not want to get caught up with her story at this time.

Gerry and I made our way into the courtroom. We took seats on the left side of the room, behind the railing that separated the criminal justice operators from the public. Stephanie Lynch, a newly hired Crime Victim Advocate from the District Attorney's Office, sat with us. She told me years later that ours was the first homicide case she was assigned. As we sat down, a dark-haired, somewhat handsome gentleman, with the build of a former football player, came over to shake our hands. It was Jim Anderson, the Assistant District Attorney. He spoke with us for a few minutes and then took his seat at one of the tables in front of the railing.

At that moment, a hefty and muscular, dark-skinned African-American man, with hair in dreadlocks, entered the room through a front side door. I realized it was International – Ralph Thomas. I had seen pictures of him in several newspaper articles. He made his way to the other table with Alameda County Deputy Public Defender James Chaffee next to him. My heart pounded; I shuddered as I thought this was the last face Mary saw on this earth. Gerry touched my arm, perhaps to help quiet my racing heart. As he took his seat, International looked towards the back of the courtroom. I am certain he saw us. I stared back, hatred leaping from my eyes.

The court officer called, "All rise," as Judge Julie Conger entered the room. When seated she glanced out over the court-room. I stared back at her intently. I wanted to make sure she saw me. My eyes told it all. "I'm here for my daughter, Mary." I desperately wanted her to know how much Mary was loved and that we would always be there for her. This meeting of eyes was enough for me; the trip was worth it.

The first witness called was Dr. John Iocco, a Forensic Pathologist with the Institute of Forensic Science. He performed autopsies on Mary and Greg on August 17. As he described Mary's wounds and the horrible condition of her body, I don't know how I sat and listened to it, without screaming. I had a yellow pad on which I took copious notes in such detail that even now I am shocked and horrified as I read them.

Some survivors want to know all there is to know about the murder so they can retrace the steps that led their loved one from this world and bear witness to their suffering. In many ways learning what happened to our loved one is a way of restor-

*ing some warmth and intimacy to their deaths, a
way of showing them that we know and care about
what happened to them. We are angry for them, sad
for them, hurt for them, proud of them, and are
there for them in their death just as we were there in
their lives."If I can stretch the arms of my empathy
around the horror my brother endured and feel his
fear and pain, then he has not died alone."*
Aftermath – In the Wake of Murder, Carrie
M. Freitag, p. 11.

I listened to the pathologist and thought, "Oh my God,
Mary, what he did to you!" Her beautiful, sweet face had been
destroyed by a gunshot wound to the right side of her neck and
an exit wound to the left side of her face, with the muzzle held
right against the skin. She had bruises to her chest inflicted by a
blunt instrument. When asked if it could have been caused by
the muzzle of a rifle, Iocco replied "Yes," to the objection of the
defense. The only consolation I derived was when he was asked,
"How long before death?" and he replied, "A matter of
moments."

Dr. Iocco described Mary's clothing: denim shorts over
running pants, a camisole and a white polo shirt, a blue sweat-
shirt, athletic socks and running shoes. Although the upper snap
of the denim shorts was undone and the zipper was partially
down, he didn't find any trauma to her private parts. I concluded that if it was a sexual assault, she must have fought like a tiger.
But even a tiger would lose to a 44-magnum rifle.

Greg's injuries appeared similar to Mary's. He had a contact gunshot wound to the left side of his neck and suffered many
bruises on his face and other parts of his body, which indicated
he too had been badly beaten by his murderer. Both Mary and
Greg had lacerations on their backs, probably from being dragged
on the pavement or dirt.

It was read into the record that Mary had a .06 blood
alcohol level and Greg's was .11, with no signs of other drugs in
either.

City of Oakland Police Officer Raymond Miller with the
Helicopter Unit was the next witness. He took Jim Anderson over
to the Berkeley Marina to take photos of the Bay area and the

landfill and marina, which were displayed at the hearing.

The story of what happened that night unfolded when James Prew was called to the witness box. To my eyes, he appeared a clean-cut young man, who lived at Rainbow Village and worked at the Berkeley Emergency Food Project. Prew identified Mary from a St. Rose College identification card. She worked at St. Rose's dining hall for a short time before going west. Prew said Mary helped out at the Food Project one day. His testimony outlined her last hours.

There was a party outside his van that night (August 15). His friends, Chris and Paul, and Greg and Mary were there. Mary was the only woman at this gathering, which did not strike me as unusual. She had five brothers and always had many male friends. International joined them and sat in the front seat of Prew's van. Greg and Mary stayed outside. Everyone was drinking and talking until about 1 am. Prew said International had "rough conversation." Anderson asked what he meant. Prew said International talked about napalm and Vietnam but didn't mention killing anyone in Vietnam. Paul told International he didn't want to hear anymore of this conversation.

A little later, at 1:25am, at Paul's suggestion, Prew drove over to Richmond to buy some more beer and burritos. Chris, Paul, International and Mary went along. Chris was dropped off at home. On the way back, Prew picked up Greg who was walking back up University Avenue. Prew drove the van back to his spot and the party continued until about 2:30am. Greg and Mary were the first to leave, telling Paul they wanted to take a walk.

Anderson asked Prew about the clothes International wore. Prew described them as dark jeans and a jacket. After International left for his car, Prew rolled up in his sleeping bag and went to sleep. He woke up at 8:30am and went over to International's lot, where he usually drank his coffee each morning. International wasn't there. When Prew drove up University Avenue to Frontage Road, he saw International next to Siebers Market, going north. Prew said International had nothing in his hand and was now wearing a yellow shirt and camouflage fatigues.

At the Public Defender's turn, he questioned Prew about the timeline in his testimony. Prew said he always wears a watch so he knew what time it was. Chaffee asked who the seven people were who were at the party. Prew responded: himself, Chris Campbell, Paul Harter, Mary, Greg, Dan, Robbie and International. They listened to music on the radio and partied about 15 minutes before International joined them. Prew said Paul and International talked about Vietnam for about 20 minutes.

Chaffee asked Prew if he saw Greg and Mary walk away. "Yes, I saw them walk towards the road out of the Village." Prew said the last time he saw Greg he wore jeans and a sarafi with lots of colors and Mary wore dark colored clothes and maybe a sleeping bag over herself.

Paul slept in Jim's van and International walked over towards his car.

Chaffee noted that when Prew spoke to Detective Eihl on August 22, he said International was wearing something dark and could have been carrying something.

Tracy Scarborough, a rather shaggy and unkempt individual, was next on the witness stand. He admitted he slept in International's car the night of the 15th, but said he was drunk and didn't know whose car he slept in. He was awakened on Friday morning about sunrise when the back hatch door slammed shut, and he saw someone going out of the Village. Everything was fuzzy because of his hangover, and he went back to sleep and woke up to the sun shining. When International came back, he said his gun, a 44 Magnum rifle, was missing and asked Tracy if he knew where it was. He had seen International with it a few weeks before and now gave him "hell" for not telling him the rifle was in the car. International told him it wasn't he who slammed the door as he had not been there all night. He was uptown in Berkeley.

Prior to a short adjournment, Jim Anderson presented a report from the U.S. Naval Observatory. On August 15, sunset was 8:02pm and on August 16, sunrise was 6:25am. As I heard this, I thought this was the first sunrise that my Mary could not see.

Tracy was back on the witness stand. The Public Defender hammered away, saying that he was so drunk he couldn't know exactly what was going on, or who slammed the hatch door. But Tracy insisted he could feel the vibration in the car. He heard International tell Harry Shorman when they went down in the direction where the body was found, "By the sounds of this, it was definitely a gun and with my record, everyone will point the finger at me."

The parade of witnesses continued. Vincent Johnson was next. A slight, frail-looking man, he lived at Rainbow Village for about 10 months and said he knew International. He gave his account of the night of August 15. He met a woman in Berkeley, earlier that day. She went down with him to his bus at the Village and stayed about two hours (midnight to 2am). When she left, Johnson drove her back to Berkeley in her car, and he walked back to the Village. He saw International at the concrete blocks with two people, a male and a female, but heard no conversation. When asked how close he got to the three, Johnson said, "about 20 feet." He hesitated when questioned how he knew it was International. He then said the man was dark-complexioned, the other two were Caucasian. International looked angry. "I didn't stop. I was going to ask if these two people needed a place to stay but since International was there, I thought he would take care of them." (*Oh, my God, if only he had walked over to them!*) Johnson said he didn't speak to them because he is shy and thought International was mad at him.

The Public Defender asked Johnson whether there had been bad feelings between himself and International. "No, just disagreements."

"You don't like each other?"

"Yes, we do, just disagreements." He said their arguments were over living conditions at Rainbow Village.

As he further described his encounter with the three, Johnson said, "Nobody spoke to me and I didn't hear anything."

Johnson said he saw nothing in anyone's hands and didn't see anyone smoke a pipe. He thought the girl was wearing a shawl. (I could picture Mary with a shawl. She owned several. I have a photo of her at her brother, Patrick's college graduation, where she had a white woolen shawl wrapped around her shoulders.)

Calvin Wiley, the next witness, owned a motor home on one of the lots and worked as a carpenter in Oakland. On the 16th, he left for work at 6:30am. On his way out of the Village, he saw International down by the weed gatherers, near the cement blocks. Wiley said International was bent over and he thought he was taking something out of the bags. International wore a pair of camouflage fatigue clothes. Wiley said he had never seen International wear those clothes before; he usually wore Levis. Wiley did not stop the car and International made no gesture to him.

The Public Defender tried to emphasize that Wiley didn't remember whether it was Thursday or Friday when he saw International down by the weed gatherers.

Thomas Midlin was the last witness. He rented the space next to International. Midlin described a scene that occurred the day before the murders. On Thursday, International sat in Midlin's station wagon cleaning his gun. They noted that Harry Shorman had a Canadian flag flying higher than an American flag on his car. When International asked Midlin if he should shoot it down, Midlin said, "Go ahead if you want to try it." Midlin later told International that he heard the shot fired from the rifle but that International had failed to hit the flag. International agreed he missed.

When the body was found, Midlin said International came to his car and told him someone had stolen his rifle. He brought over a rifle cleaning kit and asked Midlin to hold on to it.

Anderson asked Midlin, "When you talked to Detective Eihl, did you say 'hide?' "Yes," he answered.

A little later International brought over a freezer container with ammunition. Midlin heard a clunking noise so he knew there was ammunition in the container. At this point, he told International not to leave it at his place and gave him back the cleaning kit.

International told him that he had been "dumpster diving" - scrounging around through the garbage – and that he also had been back and forth from the Village five or six times. Midlin thought this was unusual because International ordinarily did not stay out all night, even going to bed earlier than the rest of them.

Anderson questioned Midlin where International did his laundry. "At the sink; same place everyone does it." Which sink? "Only sink."

The Public Defender objected when DA Anderson questioned Midlin about International's attitude toward women. Anderson argued that it pertained to two activities of the defendant that evening. One was taking his laundry to the laundromat in downtown Berkeley.

"Did he ever offer any of his attitudes toward women?"

"Mostly that they are good for cleaning up and pleasure and not much of anything else."

Anderson offered up to the Court, "Women are good for cleaning up; therefore, International would not do his own laundry." The Judge ruled part of this out.

Anderson: "Did Thomas stay with women at Rainbow Village?"

Midlin: "Yes, his girlfriend, Chris, and he were roommates. Chris has red hair and is about 5'5"."

"Did she do Ralph's laundry?"

"Yes. She did hers too. She usually took it to a laundromat and also took International's laundry."

When questioned by the Public Defender, Midlin said he was not aware of the party that night and hadn't seen Greg or Mary. The next morning International was not at Chris' space, where they usually had coffee. Midlin didn't see International until the body was found and he came to his car.

Referring to the gun cleaning kit and the ammunition, Chaffee attempted to strike the word "hide" and substitute "take care of it." But, according to Midlin, International said, "Sure, hide it under the poncho." About four or five other people also brought things to him to hold. Perhaps because he had a wife and child, it made him seem like a safe haven.

Midlin stated that he stayed at Rainbow Village every night. He couldn't see the front gate without getting out of his truck and couldn't hear outside noise very well when he was inside his truck.

When Midlin's testimony concluded, the Judge said the hearing would be continued to November 6, 1985, at 9a.m. Gerry and I were disappointed; we would not be able to be there. We were heading home the next day.

Jim Anderson then entered Ralph International Thomas' prior felony convictions into the record. In Alameda County, he was convicted of nine felony counts on 11/1/74—kidnapping, rape, oral copulation, robbery, sodomy; another count of kidnapping, robbery, rape, oral copulation. In Monterey County on 7/24/74, he was convicted of rape, a second count of rape and robbery.

When the hearing was over, a woman who had been in the back of the courtroom rushed up to speak to Gerry and me. It was Jean Stirpe, my daughter-in-law Mary Ann's aunt. Jean had been at Lawr and Mary Ann's wedding in 1982 and we met her then. Jean now lived in Oakland and had followed the case after Lawr and Mary Ann stayed with her in September while vacationing in California. Jean promised she would attend the hearing on November 6th to take notes. With Jean at the hearing, Mary would be represented once more. Over many years, Jean was my link to California and was a major player in our family's quest for justice for Mary.

After this, Gerry and I drove back to the Stearns' and filled them in on the hearing. We stayed a second night with them. Our flight home was not until the next day. We had time to do one more thing that weighed heavily on our minds. We would visit Rainbow Village and the spot where Mary drew her last breath.

The next morning, we bid farewell to Dick and Charlotte and thanked them for their kind hospitality. Gerry and I were quiet, perhaps anxious, as we drove down through Berkeley. We reached the short causeway over Route 80 to the Berkeley Marina, a small peninsula jutting out into San Francisco Bay. A hotel, with docks and sailboats behind, was located at one end; the City's landfill, with Rainbow Village adjacent, was at the farther end. A narrow body of water separated the City of Berkeley from the landfill area.

When we arrived at Rainbow Village we saw about 30 vehicles parked on rather small sites. There were small pick-up trucks with camper shells, abandoned school buses decorated with curtains and stained glass windows, and several sub-compact cars. The Village residents appeared resourceful; some used potbelly stoves for heat and rechargeable batteries powered their televisions. There was running water, and several outhouses were conspicuous. A small intimate community was being developed there.

On the road into the Village, we met Claus von Wendel, the captain of a home built boat, which he told us was being prepared to sail around the world. The boat, *The Sea Space Station*, was docked in the inlet. Von Wendel knew about the murders and had reported to the police that someone left a bag on his boat that night. He thought someone may have been trying to set him up and that the missing rifle may have been in this bag. When he opened it, he found no evidence of a gun.

After we parked our car, we ran into Harry Shorman, the self-anointed spokesperson for the Village. A short man, with long, dark hair and a mustache, he gave us several of his hand-outs. One was the "magna carta" for Rainbow Village, dated 1-27-85, containing 21 residents' names and the makes and models of their vehicles. The other was a "Vehicle Dweller Newspaper," dated 10/18/85, which outlined happenings at the Village.

Having heard yesterday's testimony, we made our way to the spot where we believed Mary and Greg were beaten and shot. As we stood at the rocky slope leading down to the narrow inlet, I envisioned Mary and Greg sitting there looking over at the hills and lights of Berkeley. It was a very difficult moment for both Gerry and me, one filled with unspeakable pain. We held on to one another, sobbing. Through the tears, my thoughts framed a prayer to my daughter, and promised that we would always be her voice, crying out for justice for her murder. And as the tears subsided, my resolve was even deeper, harder than before.

We stayed at the site for a little while, remembering Mary as we always would—a joyful, loving, concerned young woman who did not deserve to die so young. Then we turned and walked back to the car. I couldn't help feeling that we were leaving a bit of Mary back there at the Berkeley Marina.

Gerry and I were quiet on the ride out of the Village and over to the Oakland airport. It had been a tough few days that we would always remember. On the trip home, the flight attendants wore colorful, spooky masks, and made playful announcements over the speakers. After all, it was a holiday – Halloween - and life goes on.

14

THE PRELIMINARY HEARING CONTINUES

Jean Stirpe, true to her word, attended the continuation of the Preliminary Hearing on November 6th and sent me her detailed notes. As I read them, I am once again back in the Berkeley Municipal Courthouse.

The two detectives who worked on our case were called first. Detective Fred Eihl was at the scene as Mary was brought in from the water. A crowd of onlookers from the Village immediately gathered. He held them back from interfering with the crime scene. Although it was not known if the body recovered was male or female, Eihl heard a man, later identified as International, say, "That's Mary." At the time, he was 25 feet from the body. Eihl asked International how he knew Mary. "Washed dishes with her at the Village." He told Eihl she had come into the Village a few days before and he had been at a party with her.

Eihl described the scenario International gave to the police about that night. After the party broke up, he went into town for liquor. On the way, he saw Mary and Greg on the concrete blocks next to the water, and they asked him for a match. He stayed with them and smoked dope. When he got to the liquor store, it was closed so he went back to the Village and got whiskey from the car. He also got some money and went back again to Berkeley looking to "score some dope." At daybreak, he walked back to the Village, got his laundry and went up to Berkeley to the laundromat. When he arrived back at the Village, he heard a body was found. International told the police he walked to all these places. The police calculated the round trip distances: 4.4 miles to liquor store; 8.8 miles to get the dope at Durant & Telegraph, 3.6 miles to laundromat. Total mileage: 16.8 miles.

The Public Defender countered that in Eihl's written police report International said "That looks like Mary," not "That's Mary." He pointed out that Eihl had not questioned International about the night's timeline and how long it took him to walk back and forth from the Village to Berkeley.

Jean's notes were lengthy on the testimony of Inspector Dan Wolke, the next witness. When Wolke arrived at the scene, the other officers, including Eihl, were already there. The body had been removed from the water. A large photo of the area where Mary was found was displayed on a board for all in the courtroom to see. Wolke remained at the Village for the next five or six hours. He said a pipe was found later that day just west of the sand pile.

The next day, August 17, he went back with a scuba diving team. They did a hand-over-hand search in the water and found the second body, Greg Kniffin. Wolke described Greg as having brown hair and a beard, and he was wearing bib overalls and white socks.

Wolke later went over to space 24 at the Village to interview International, who was in a blue Opal Cadet car. International told Wolke he met Mary Thursday morning washing dishes outside the fence. She stayed in the Blunder bus (Grateful Dead fans used it to stay in between shows). On the night of the 15th, Mary and Greg called to him, asked if he had marijuana, and all three smoked out of his pipe. He thought he still had the pipe but must have lost it or left it with Mary and Greg. (A pipe and a girl's watch, still working, were found near the drag marks next to the sand pile.) International told Wolke that when Vincent Johnson walked by, Mary and Greg were very happy; Mary was dancing.

Wolke asked International whether he knew if anyone at the Village had guns. He said he would rather not say because some people there might be on parole and should not have a firearm. International then told Wolke he owned a Remington rifle, which was stolen possibly on Thursday afternoon but didn't report it to the police because of his parole status. He said it was a clip-fed rifle and was able to give the serial number from memory.

International told Wolke he would go down to the police department the next day to make an official report about the gun. When he was there, International said the last time he fired the gun was on the 15th, when he shot at Harry Shorman's flag. He cleaned the rifle, put it in a case with ten to eleven bullets in a plastic container, covered it with a blanket, and placed it back behind the seats in his car. After that, he drank beer with Tracy Scarborough, who fell asleep in his car.

International repeated the story about the party at Jim Prew's van to Wolke and his trip to the liquor store to buy beer. But International said when Vince Johnson saw him with Mary and Greg, Vince said hello. (Vince Johnson's testimony was that he did not speak to International when he saw him.) International gave Wolke some names of people he met on his trip back to the Village with his laundry. He said when he put the laundry in the back of his car, the rifle case was there, but the rifle and the container with bullets were missing. He spoke to Tracy about the missing rifle and then heard that a body was found.

Wolke testified that when he asked International at the scene, "Why would anyone want to kill the victim? he replied, 'There are many reasons why someone would want to kill them.'" When Wolke asked him what they were, International couldn't think of any then. Wolke then suggested that he should take a polygraph test pertaining to the missing rifle. International refused, saying he needed counsel and asked him for the location of the Public Defender's office.

Jim Anderson, "Was International a suspect before this interview?"

Wolke replied, "No, but after the 'Many reasons…' statement and some other inconsistencies, he was."

On August 27th, International's car and space behind it were searched by the police.

The Public Defender pointed out several inconsistencies when he questioned Wolke: Thomas' work boots didn't match the footprints in the dirt at the scene and insisted again that International said, "That looks like Mary."

Chaffee called upon Harry Shorman to clarify what

International said when Mary was brought in from the water. Shorman said International stated he thought it was Mary because of the purple leggings and other clothing that he had seen her wear at the party.

Countering this, Jim Anderson showed the picture of Mary in the water. He questioned whether Shorman would have been able to see the leggings and their color as they were standing eleven feet from the shoreline and the body was 6 feet farther out in the water. Shorman admitted International seemed tense when he said, "Oh, that looks like Mary" and said he had partied with her the night before.

Jean noted that the hearing concluded at 4pm. The Judge announced that she would visit the site, along with the attorneys and Detective Eihl, to clarify locations. The hearing would resume the next day.

Jean could not attend when Vivian Cercey appeared at the Preliminary Hearing the next afternoon. Cercey's testimony from the court record is summarized below.

In the early hours of August 16th , Cercey was in the vicinity of Rainbow Village, having arrived late the night before. Harry Shorman was an "on and off" boyfriend so she stayed there a few times. She had two young daughters, ages four and one. With no permanent home, she lived out of her brown 1973 Dodge.

On August 15, Cercey parked her car at the end of the road outside Rainbow Village. Around 1:30am (August 16), she went to the dumpster to clean out the trash in her car. She saw three people, one woman and two men, standing by a bus and an orange and red van. The woman looked upset. One of the men had blonde hair, and he and the girl seemed to be having an argument. Cercey saw a long stick, which, in later testimony, she said might be a gun. The girl said, "You have to give it back," but the blonde man said, "This could mean money to us; we need this." The girl said, "I don't want any part of this. I'm going." When she walked away, she passed Cercey, who invited her in and told her she didn't have to take this "shit," but she said she would be all right and kept walking. Cercey heard the blonde man say he would take care of this and walked past her car in the same direction as the girl. Cercey asked him his name but he didn't answer. He seemed to be carrying something but she couldn't tell if it was a weapon.

Cercey drove back to where she had been parked. About 15 minutes later, she heard what sounded like three firecrackers. She went to sleep and later saw a man who looked similar to the blonde man come up from the waterfront. He wiped his hands on the vegetation. Afterward when Cercey went up to Harry's spot, she saw a man washing his hair and hands at the sink outside the Village gate. She thought he threw something into the fence. A little later, a man knocked at her car window and he asked her where she was staying. She mentioned Harry's name, and the man asked who he was. Cercey asked why he was asking all these questions, and the man said because I am going to kill you. She said it had to be about 4am. The man walked away and she stayed frozen at the spot until she left to give someone a ride to work.

DA Anderson then questioned about her ability to see what she said she witnessed. Cercey said it was a "pretty light night. No fog, no smoke. Pretty visible evening." Anderson asked her if she was intoxicated that night. She replied no; she had about four beers from Noon until 11pm. He then questioned whether she had ever asked police for protection. She said no and also said she had not asked Shorman to ask for police protection for her.

With the conclusion of Vivian Cercey's testimony, the Preliminary Hearing ended.

After considering all the testimony in the hearing, Judge Conger determined there was sufficient evidence to send the case on to Alameda County Superior Court for trial.

On November 25, 1985, papers were filed in that Court, charging Ralph International Thomas with the murders of Mary Gioia and Gregory Kniffin and alleged special circumstances (multiple murders) and the use of a firearm. In addition, the twelve prior felony convictions were entered: in Monterey County (June 26, 1974), two for rape and one for robbery; in Alameda County (November 3, 1974), two for simple kidnapping; two for rape; two for oral copulation, two for robbery and one for sodomy.

On December 5, 1985, International pled not guilty to the murders, denied the special circumstances, and was mute on the prior convictions. The trial would begin in May.

15

THE TRIAL BEGINS

Sunday, May 11, 1986 - Mother's Day. Joan and I—two mothers—prepare to leave for California. At 11am, Mike brought Joan over to the house. Amanda, their cute, curly-haired three-year-old held on to her Mom. She knew something big was happening and didn't want to let go of her. Lawr and Mary Ann were already there.

"Well, I guess this is it," I said, looking anxiously at everyone. "Jim Anderson hasn't called to tell us of any delays so it must be safe to be on our way."

We walked out onto the back porch. Dan waited for us at the car. He was home after just completing his sophomore year. He volunteered to be our chauffeur, driving us down to Newark Airport to catch the People's Express flight. After many hugs and kisses from everyone, and a few tears hurriedly wiped away, we began our trip. Dan very ably maneuvered through all the traffic on the New Jersey Turnpike to reach the airport.

Our flight was at 4pm. When we arrived at the People's Express terminal, Dan took our bags from the trunk of the car. He hugged us, his eyes brimming over with tears. Yes, even tough football players can show their feelings. "It'll be okay, Mom. Mary's with you guys. Call and keep us updated."

After final hugs, Joan said, "I'll take care of Mom. We'll be all right."

Joan was six months pregnant with her second child. She checked with her doctor to be certain she could make the trip. It would be an emotional one for her; she was the last family mem-

124

ber to see Mary before she left for California.

Joan wrote a detailed summary of the trip in her diary and shared much of it with me. It helped with many of the details of our stay.

Our plane arrived in San Francisco at 7pm. Jean Stirpe was there to meet us, as she often would when the rest of the family came out to California.

"Welcome to San Francisco and California," she said as she gave us each a bear hug. "Wish it could be for a happier occasion."

From the airport, Jean drove over the San Francisco-Oakland Bay Bridge to Oakland. As I looked out the car window at the water on either side, my mind jumped to Mary. For several years I was unable to look at a lakefront or beach without it bringing forth images of Mary, found floating in the Bay waters.

We had dinner in a restaurant in Oakland before heading up to Jean's home. She lived on Skyline Boulevard, which skirted several regional parklands. Her house was on one of the highest points in Oakland. As Jean navigated the long and winding road, there were many homes, some small, some large, built along the side of this road. As we kept going upward, I smiled and asked Jean if she supplied oxygen masks for her visitors.

When we finally reached Skyline Boulevard, Jean parked in the carport directly behind her house. The house was built into the side of a hill and had several levels. Our bedroom window in the back of the house had a splendid view of the City of Oakland, the Golden Gate Bridge and the Bay. It was a spectacular sight, especially at night when the lights of the city and bridge could be seen. The three of us sat and talked a short time before heading off to bed and our first night's sleep in Oakland.

Monday, May 12 - We awoke about 6:30 am to the sound of coffee beans being ground in the kitchen, a culinary practice that Jean passed on to me. After breakfast, she drove us down, down the long hill to the main district of Oakland. We were headed for the Alameda County Court House, a cream-colored stone building, which encompassed the entire block of 12th and Oak Streets. It would soon become all too familiar to us. Jean dropped us off in front of the courthouse. Employed as a graphics artist, she had to go to work but promised to pick us up later that day.

Joan and I walked into the lobby of the courthouse. We felt lost. Everyone else seemed to know what they were doing, where they were going. Youthful, energetic lawyers, with brief-cases in tow, chatted with one another and waited for the elevator. We asked where the District Attorney's office was located, and then took the elevator up to it. Jim Anderson waited for us. David Kniffin, Greg's dad, was already there. His sister, Dorothy Vickers, and her former husband, Bill, were with him.

After brief introductions, Jim filled us in on what already took place. They were in the midst of jury selection, begun the week before. Following our orientation, we all headed down to the Jury Assembly Room, where twelve jurors and four alternates were to be chosen.

When jury selection was completed, there were six women and six men. The alternates were two women and two men. I jotted down some of their occupations as I heard them read - a G.E. employee; a housewife; medical equipment and insurance field workers; an industrial ceramics worker; an accountant; a mechanic; a high school band leader; a lab technologist; a truck driver; a financial analyst, and a data processor. It certainly was a varied group.

With jury selection completed, we were free until afternoon. Joan, David, Dorothy, Bill and I went to lunch at MaryAnn's Sandwich Shop near the courthouse. A simple luncheon café, with a few tables, it became our haunt and relief each day of the trial. This was a time to get acquainted with the other victim's family; they had not attended the Preliminary Hearing. David and I had spoken by telephone several times over the months before the trial, but this was our first face to face meeting. As I recall, it seemed almost bizarre. Here we were eating and talking - two families tied into the same terrible circumstances - the murder of a son, the murder of a daughter.

David appeared to be a father in deep pain. His only son, murdered. He and David's mother had gone to Berkeley to identify Greg after the police found him. It must have been a dreadful, horrific moment. I thought of our decision not to go out to California to identify Mary. Nobody's right or wrong at such a time. One has to do what one's own heart tells them is best.

I felt David harbored some anger that Greg had left his home without finishing high school. Such a decision may have been even more troubling to David, a graduate of Wharton Business School, with a good job in New York City. Greg's mother, Judy, did not attend the trial. Several years later she visited me over lunch in my home. We talked about our kids—two mothers with broken hearts. I think Judy felt she could not handle the agony of sitting through the trial, hearing details of what had happened to her precious son. Her young daughter lived with her in Pennsylvania and also needed her. David was fortunate to have a sister and brother-in-law living nearby in San Jose for family support during the trials.

At lunch, Dorothy and Bill made an incredible offer to Joan and me. They noted Jean dropped us off on her way to work. They proposed that we borrow one of their two automobiles for the length of the trial, a Volkswagen "bug" or a second larger car. I was stunned. When I collected my wits, I told them I couldn't imagine depriving them of their larger car but we would gladly borrow the VW if they didn't need it during that time. Coincidentally, the first car owned by our family was a VW "bug;" so I thought I could be reasonably comfortable driving one again. They promised we would have it the next day. Our family will never forget their generosity. It allowed Joan and me, and the others who came out later, to be able to move around the area independently.

After lunch, we traipsed back to the courthouse as the opening arguments began. This courtroom was similar to the one in the Berkeley courthouse but larger. There were more rows for observers. Joan and I, with David and his family next to us, all filed into the front row on the left—the People's side. As we sat there, we heard Jim Anderson, with his usual passion and fervor, outline the facts he would present to the jury in the coming days.

Nobody saw him commit the crimes, Anderson told the jury, but when you hear all the evidence, there's no rational explanation except that Ralph Thomas is guilty. <u>Daily Californian</u>, 5/13/86.

The Public Defender Chaffee presented counter arguments focusing on the lack of incriminating physical evidence and concluded, *The evidence is not sufficient beyond a reasonable doubt to prove Mr. Thomas is guilty.* <u>Daily Californian</u>, 5/13/86.

Joan wrote in her journal: "Saw International from the

start of the trial – he was sitting so close we could've thrown things at him! Looks big and mean." Yes, I'm sure Joan was taken aback, as I was, by the first sight of this man who murdered her sister and changed our family's lives forever.

In her impact letter to Judge Byers, Joan expressed the pain she experienced on learning of her sister's murder:

> I am the oldest of the eight children in the Gioia family. We are all very close and have become even more so since the death of our father in 1977. I remember expressing to my mother at the time of my Dad's death that I would always be around to help anyone in the family if it was needed.
>
> The youngest two in the family, Mary and Daniel, were only 14 and 11 years old, respectively, at the time of Dad's death. I felt as though I especially needed to take them under my wing and always be there for them if they needed me. I took them to baseball games at Yankee Stadium with my friends and helped both of them get their auto licenses....I tried to pay attention to what was going on with them through their high school and college years.
>
> There is nothing I wouldn't do for my sister, Mary, and so in the fall of 1984, when she asked to come and live with me and my husband, Mike, and daughter, Amanda, for a while, I accepted her and her cat, Samson, with open arms. I am glad we had those months together to grow even closer and yet it made it almost even harder for me to accept her death.
>
> The effect of my sister Mary's death on me has certainly been a somber one. I have continued on with my life—trying to be a good wife and a good mom. I am also a registered nurse and work in an emergency room. I have continued to work, and though it was very difficult at first to concentrate on my job and its responsibilities, I have persevered and still receive satisfaction from my job.
>
> I talk to my family, my friends, and Mary's

*friends every once in a while about Mary and it
helps me to do so. I will always love my little sister,
Mary, just as I love my other sister, Chris, and my
five brothers. I just know she is happy in Heaven
with our Dad, and I am glad that she can no longer
be hurt anymore. The rest of us live on with the
hurt, but we remember all the good times and the
loving girl that Mary was...She was a really beautiful person who deserves to still be walking around
on this earth, and certainly did not deserve to be
murdered.*

Tuesday, May 13 - David and I were the first witnesses
called to the stand. The Public Defender tried to have our testimony excluded as irrelevant and prejudicial, arguing it was likely to prejudice the jury. The judge overruled him, saying our purpose would be to identify the victims and testify how long and
for what reason they were in Berkeley. We were not to testify as
to their character; but simply state what they were doing in
California.

As the trial developed, I learned that the Public Defender,
International's attorney, would do any and almost everything to
defend his client. Although, as victims' families, we may dislike
their tactics, it is the job of the defense attorney to raise every
possible motion and argument to protect the defendant's interests. This became evident as Jim Chaffee tried to block our statements.

I realized this would be a very important moment for me,
my only chance to speak for Mary in that courtroom. Doris Aiken
and other advocates back home suggested that I bring a large
photo of Mary with me. As I spoke, it was displayed for everyone
to see—a beautiful, young woman cut down in her prime. After
I was sworn in, I took my seat in the witness box. My heart flut-
tered as I looked out at my audience: the judge, the jury, the two
attorneys on either side of our case, the court stenographer, a few
observers, and Ralph International Thomas. I secretly whispered
to Mary, "Okay, now you've got to help me get through this."

Jim Anderson: "Mrs. Gioia, tell us what Mary was doing
out here in California."

I took a deep breath and began, "Mary was the seventh of my eight children. She had a dream. She wanted to see the west coast. Many of her friends and acquaintances had come out here. She wrote me a letter, posted August 13th from Oakland. I was reading it when the police arrived at my home. She said she was going up and down the coast, trying to decide where she might find work."

Taking another deep breath, I continued, "Mary had a degree in culinary arts from our local community college. She was a fantastic baker. Her letter mentioned various places where she might find work in a restaurant or in a resort."

At that, the Judge looked over at me, interrupted my story, and politely thanked me. I felt like I had just begun to let everyone know who Mary Regina Gioia was. However, I quickly realized that in the court's eyes, I was finished. I do not recall being cross-examined by the Public Defender. I left the witness box and left the courtroom.

David's testimony was next. I didn't stay to hear it, as we had arranged to meet outside the courthouse after our testimony. We knew the Forensic Pathologist would be called after this and we did not want to be in the courtroom to hear him. I had already sat through it once at the Preliminary Hearing.

David testified that Greg was the older of his two children. David had a photograph of Greg, which was displayed while he was on the stand. He told the court that after he and his wife divorced, Greg became depressed, lost interest in school and dropped out. In June of 1985, he quit his job and traveled across the country to California in a bus, hoping to find work. In his last telephone call to David, Greg told him he liked California and hoped to stay there. At the conclusion of David's testimony, the two victims had been identified.

Dr. John Iocco, the Forensic Pathologist, was the next witness and testified about the condition of Mary and Greg's bodies when they were brought in from the Bay waters. While he was on the stand, David, Joan and I sat outside the courthouse, talking. Everything still seemed so unreal. Do you ever get used to being at your child's murder trial?

My mind must have been consumed with this thought, as I wrote in my notebook words from the depth of my very soul.

130

Mary, I can never suffer as you did. But right now, my suffering is almost as great. Someday, my sweetheart, there will be justice, and this man will be away so he can't hurt anyone again. Mary, I love you. I hope the jurors have been affected by these pictures—first, you and Greg as you were— happy in life—and then as he left you.

Lieutenant Miller of the Oakland City Police, the next witness, stated that sunset was 8:02 pm on August 15 and sunrise was 6:25 am on August 16.

After lunch, we were back in the courtroom. Inspector Dan Wolke, in charge of Homicide for 8 1/2 years, the next witness, reviewed for both Anderson and Chaffee all the places International told police he traveled to and from in the early hours of August 16th. A large map displayed in the courtroom traced these supposed trips, showing approximate mileage. After Wolke's testimony concluded, court adjourned for the day.

We had some free time so Joan and I accompanied David, Dorothy and Bill over to Rainbow Village, a difficult visit for all, but especially for Joan. She now saw for the first time where her little sister was murdered. Driving into the Village, we stopped to speak to Claus von Wendel, the captain of the boat docked at the estuary. Even though all of the other residents were gone, he remained at the Bay in his boat, getting it ready for his round-the-world trip.

Rainbow Village, now closed, contained a few remnants as reminders of the community once forged there. Discarded furniture and a wooden "PEACE" sign lay next to a closed barbedwire fence. Another sign reading "VILLAGE" was propped up against a closed wooden fence, and a bus was parked in the wideopen space where the Villagers' vehicles had once been. I wondered if this was one of the Deadhead buses parked there last year. A large boulder was propped next to a fence. On it, someone scrawled in blue letters, "Rainbow Village was here 1-31-85 – 3-3-86." Yes, Rainbow Village was no more.

Over that year, Jean kept me informed with news clips that told the story of Rainbow Village's demise. In January 1986, the Berkeley City Council ruled that Rainbow Village had to be

131

dismantled by March 3rd. The City faced losing $760,000 in state and federal money for development of a park at the site if the Village was not disbanded on that date. The State Land Commission and the Marriott Hotel, which had an inn on the Marina, won their lawsuit claiming the land belonged to the public and could not be used for residential purposes. The City had until March to find another site for the Village. Finding none, all the residents had to move out - some going to homeless shelters, some receiving help in federally subsidized housing, and some just moving on.

We stayed for about an hour. Having heard some of the trial testimony, it meant more to see the area now. Joan and I, arm in arm, walked down the dirt path from the vacated Village to the road near the water.

Joan asked me, "Do you think this is where Mary and Greg were sitting when International came upon them?"

"I don't know but it looks like the spot where Vincent Johnson saw them. They must have been looking over at the hills of Berkeley and the lights from the houses there. It's hard to imagine what they thought when International came upon them."

Joan started to cry and we both hugged each other. I managed to spurt out, "Perhaps it's best not to speculate on those last moments. I know I wouldn't be able to go on if I concentrated on that. We have to remember Mary as we knew her, our sweet, innocent Mary."

We joined the others and headed back to Oakland. There the light-colored VW bug awaited us in the parking garage across from the courthouse. After we received a few directives and general instructions about the car from Dorothy and Bill, we set out for Jean's. It was definitely a test for me as I was not used to driving any car but my own. With a pregnant daughter as my passenger, I was cautious. I drove toward the Oakland hills but each cross street I came to appeared to lead upwards.

"We'll just have to take a chance on one of these," I said, realizing that this was the only way to get back to Jean's. Suddenly, I spied, "Brooklyn Street."

"Sounds good; let's go." But even that street with its comforting name for a New Yorker was the start of a long hill. When we finally reached the road leading up to Skyline Drive, I put the car in second gear, gunned the motor of the bug, and we made it!

Jean was as usual anxious to hear about what happened that day in court. After dinner we sat around, wine glasses in hand (except Joan), and reviewed the day's events with her.

16

THE TRIAL CONTINUES

Wednesday, May 14 – Today the jury visited Rainbow Village. International went along; we didn't. It might look as if we were hounding him if we were there too. Court would be delayed.

With our own wheels, we drove down to the courthouse in the afternoon. When David and Dorothy spotted us in the garage, they asked, "How was the Bug? Any problems?"

"No, it's great. The hills were a challenge at first but I'm determined to get used to them. I can't tell you how much I appreciate the use of the car."

We made our way into the courtroom and filed into our seats. Jim Anderson called his first witness, David Bergman, also known as "Mousey." He lived at Rainbow Village for three months and was its Postmaster. It was the first time I saw Bergman; he was not a witness called when Gerry and I attended the Preliminary Hearing.

Bergman testified that he drove International to the liquor store on August 15, and that around 7pm that night, when he was in his camper watching television, he heard a gunshot hit a vehicle. When International told him he shot at the Canadian flag on Harry Shorman's car with a Remington Model 788, 44 Magnum rifle, Bergman told him it was a stupid thing to do. He also testified that he saw International with the rifle about a month before when he used it for target practice on some cans.

When Bergman went to the outhouse, at about 10pm on the 15th, he said he saw International. At that point, Anderson asked him if there were any lights in the Village, to which Bergman replied there were none - only candles, headlights and kerosene lamps. And after sunset, visibility was only about 10 to 15 feet on the road.

Bergman also testified that he suggested to International the following day that he should report his missing rifle to the police when International told him it was missing.

At the Public Defender's turn, he asked Bergman about "groupies," who stayed at the Village. Bergman described the Blunder Bus as where the groupies (followers of the Grateful Dead) would stay. And he said additional groupies stayed on the "Dead On" bus, which its owner, Randy, parked outside the gate. Bergman estimated there were a minimum of five, a maximum of 20, Grateful Dead followers at Rainbow Village on August 15.

The DA's next two witnesses, Calvin Wiley and Tracy Scarborough, gave testimony that I heard previously at the Preliminary Hearing. Chaffee now wanted the jury to consider others who might have been responsible for the murders so he asked Tracy if he knew about the "Troll Patrol." These were local vigilantes from the Santa Cruz area whose usual victims were hippie types. My notes do not indicate Tracy's response to this but the insinuation was now out there.

Chaffee introduced a discussion about International's car because Tracy slept in it that night. It had a broken window on the driver's side and a pile of "stuff" on the back seat, which could be reached from outside. I wrote, *Good point. International could have gotten his gun that way.*

Jim Prew was the last witness called. His testimony closely followed that given at the Preliminary Hearing. Mary volunteered to work at the Berkeley Emergency Food Project on the 14th but didn't work there on the 15th. This was one of the happy images I had of her last days. I'm sure whatever her assignment at the Food Project was she did well and in a caring manner.

Prew said Mary came into the Drop In Center at the University Lutheran Chapel on the 15th and after work he met up with Greg and Mary and several others. They all went down to Rainbow Village. He again described the party scene outside his van; most drank beer but International drank whiskey. At 3am, the party broke up. Anderson asked who left first, and he said Greg and Mary left together to take a walk in the field;

International left after that. Prew's friend, Paul, stayed and they both slept in the van. Prew awakened at 8:30am and went over to International's space but International wasn't there. When he saw him later at the Sea Breeze Market, International wore a yellow shirt and camouflage pants.

At the conclusion of Prew's testimony, court was over for the day. David, Dorothy, Joan and I took a little side excursion to Jack London Square, nearby. We needed a break from the intensity of the courtroom drama. The area dated back to gold rush days when, as a young boy, Jack London, sold newspapers at this spot. There he collected many stories from seafarers, which he used in his later writings including The Call of the Wild. I particularly liked our tour of the First and Last Chance Saloon and London's Yukon cabin; at least I gleaned some history of the area I now found myself at. We dined at one of the restaurants at the Square. Joan's journal entry described the long day well. She wrote, "Didn't get home until past ten that night. I was exhausted!"

Thursday – May 15 – We were back in court. It was now the Public Defender's turn to cross-examine Jim Prew, who retold how he took Chris Campbell home to Richmond. On the way back to the Village, International kidded about Prew's driving, offering to teach him how to drive. Hearing this, I surmised the defense wanted to paint International as a "nice guy."

Vincent Johnson, the next witness, repeated his story about accompanying his woman friend back up to Berkeley, also told at the Preliminary Hearing. There were no lights on the road as he walked back to the Village. When he passed the landfill office, he saw three people next to the first set of cement pilings: a young Caucasian female, a young Caucasian male and a Black male. He didn't hear any voices. He was about 15 to 20 feet away from them. He kept walking. He recognized International, who just stood there, staring into space. They did not make eye contact but it looked like International was mad, upset. Jim Anderson reminded Johnson that he previously said, "angry and pissed off." Johnson said he did not know Greg and Mary. He continued to walk back to his bus, where he retired. He said he heard nothing more.

The Public Defender in his cross-examination, asked about International.

"You and he did not get along. You didn't like him."

Johnson replied, "No, I didn't dislike him."

When Chaffee cross-examined Johnson, he insinuated Johnson was upset with International because he didn't want the Midlins to move in as it would be too crowded with so many vehicles close together.

It was difficult to listen to Johnson's testimony. From where I sat, this man was the only one, if he acted differently, who might have saved Mary and Greg. If he had gone over to speak to International, perhaps they could have escaped harm.

Thomas Midlin, the next witness, said he lived at Rainbow Village since April 1985 and hung out with International and his woman friend, Chris, most of the time. His daughter, Harmony, and wife, Melody, lived with him.

On August 16, after the body was found, International told Midlin his rifle was missing. He told him to call the police. When International asked him to hold on to the cleaning kit and the Tupperware case with ammunition, he told International, "I don't want these things around."

Midlin said International liked to play "Stalk, where he would creep up on somebody, preferably in the dark, when they did not know he was there."

In cross-examination, the Public Defender tried to portray a "nice guy" image again for International when Midlin said his daughter, Harmony, would go down to International and Chris' spot and they would take care of her and feed her.

Jim Anderson called upon Fred Eihl after Midlin's testimony concluded. Eihl, a police officer with the City of Berkeley, had only worked on homicide cases since July 1985. He went down to Rainbow Village when Mary was found and retold the conversation he had with International at the scene when International said, "That's Mary." At the rocks near the water, he observed the blood and drag marks over the grass from the road, and he recovered a corn cob pipe.

He spoke to Robin Van Heest and learned more about Mary and Greg from him. He looked for the others who were at the party and eventually interviewed Paul Harter, Chris Campbell, Jim Prew and Cho (who stayed on the "Dead-On" bus).

After Greg was found, Eihl observed the autopsies. He

placed some of Mary's things in a bag (probably for evidence), including matchboxes from some restaurants in California. Hearing that, I thought she probably wanted them as souvenirs to show us when she returned home.

Eihl said he was at the Hall of Justice (city jail) when International was arrested and checked for bites, cuts and bruises.

He said Vincent Johnson came to the Police Department voluntarily as he had rethought the time he was with the woman, Betty Jo. It was not 1am, more likely 2am.

Inspector Dan Wolke was the last witness that day. His testimony centered on his interview with International regarding the party at Jim's van, seeing Mary and Greg later when Vince Johnson walked by, and his many trips up to Berkeley for liquor, dope and to do his laundry. Wolke further testified that International told him that when he later walked back where Mary and Greg had been, he didn't see them.

When the court session was over, the Judge announced there would be none the next day. We would be free until Monday.

Heading over to the garage, David asked, "Since there's no court, would you like to have a tour of San Francisco and the surrounding area tomorrow?"

"We'd love to. Joan, do you agree?"

"Sure. I'll be heading home on Monday and since this is my first trip west, that would be great."

We made arrangements to meet David the next day at the courthouse garage. On the way home, we stopped at Jean's favorite supermarket and picked up some food for dinner. Jean had been very generous but we wanted to carry our own weight too.

Friday – May 16 - David met us in Oakland in the morning. He had been to California before so he was our chauffeur and tour guide for the day.

We drove across the five-lane, two-level San Francisco-Oakland Bay Bridge, which connects the East Bay to the City of San Francisco. We were excited about our visit to this remarkable City, which is built on hills. It has about 43 of them and is at the tip of a peninsula surrounded by San Francisco Bay and the Pacific Ocean. As we drove through busy streets, I pictured Mary, our country girl, perhaps a bit perplexed by the hustle and bustle of this place, yet eager to try it out and become a part of it.

When we arrived at Golden Gate Park, the largest man-made park in the world, we stopped at the Japanese Tea Garden. Our lagging spirits were suddenly rejuvenated when we saw all its beautiful, well-tended, sculptured plants. Leaving there, the Pacific Ocean was right next to us. We parked the car and walked around. I couldn't help feeling minuscule, next to the vastness of this magnificent ocean. Back in the car, we drove around the Presidio, viewing the remnants of the military barracks and brick fortress that once guarded the Golden Gate area during the Civil War.

We were now at the Golden Gate Bridge, painted its distinctive orange color. David drove the 1.7 miles across the bridge to Marin County. We toured the picturesque Mediterranean-style village of Sausalito, its streets peppered with Victorian bungalows and little shops. We stopped along Bridgeway Avenue at one of its many restaurants and had a relaxing lunch. Joan and I were getting to know David better as we had plenty of time to talk about our families, our kids, our lives - and in a more relaxed atmosphere than the Oakland courthouse. After lunch, we headed back to Oakland. Jean, away for the weekend visiting one of her daughters, left us to our own wits in California!

On Saturday, Joan and I were still in the tourist mood. We decided to drive over to San Francisco again. We took advantage of having our own transportation, to be able to go where we wanted. After breakfast, we headed down through Oakland, with its famous Mormon Temple in our sights, towards the San Francisco-Oakland Bay Bridge. It was my first attempt to drive on this monstrous bridge but, with Joan's encouragement, I did it. Bridges have always been a problem for me - perhaps because of my fear of heights!

Once in San Francisco, we took a quick motor tour of some of its famous neighborhoods. We drove down Bryant Street and spied the Hall of Justice (oh, how that resonated with us). Next we headed over to Market Street and to the Civic Center. City Hall was quite impressive and our guide books told us that its grand Baroque dome was modeled after St. Peter's in Rome. It's even higher than our Capitol's in Washington, D.C.

We stopped for a few minutes to collect our thoughts and read our maps. We knew what we were looking for. In Mary's letter, she told me a friend said she could use the address, 1906 McAllister Street, to receive mail, and she could use it as an address for job applications. She wrote: "This is how my friend Mike told me how to remember it – Just remember the year of the Earthquake – 1906 – Lovin' that one!" We drove along Van Ness Avenue, alongside City Hall, and we were at McAllister. Our eyes searched for 1906. We did not find it and Joan said she thinks we missed it too. So we never connected with anyone, or "Mike," who might have given us more information about Mary's last days out there.

We continued driving through the hilly streets of Nob Hill and saw the famous San Francisco cable cars. We passed the "Crookedest Street in the World," on our way to Fisherman's Wharf, but did not attempt to drive down it. At the Wharf, we parked the Bug and walked along the streets lined with restaurants, shops and amusements venues of all kinds. We stopped to observe the sea lions basking on Pier 39's wharf. Their wails almost sounded human as they slumped along some of the docks. We meandered over to Ghiradelli Square and enjoyed the sights at the former chocolate factory and woolen mill and bought some gifts for those at home. We sat for a while, resting and gazing at the other tourists, probably here for a visit, not as we were, to attend a murder trial. My thoughts, as always, wandered to Mary—how excited she must have been to see all these places we've now seen - on a trip we would never have chosen to make.

After a while, we were hungry. Joan, who loves Chinese food, suggested that we head over to San Francisco's famous Chinatown. We chose a restaurant, not for its fame or culinary ability, but because we finally found a parking space. The sidewalks were very crowded as we made our way into the restaurant. There we enjoyed a genuine Chinese meal, taking home some leftovers. Tired after our day's outing, we headed back over the Bay Bridge to Oakland and up to Skyline Blvd.

The next day, Sunday, was another day of rest for Joan and me. It had been a long, tiring, and emotional week. There was so much to talk and mull over since the trial had been on all week. That afternoon, we drove down the hill to the grocery store to purchase food and a few supplies. Then, it must have been that pregnant craving of Joan's, but we wound up getting

Chinese take-out for dinner!

When Jean arrived back that evening, there were lots of adventures to tell her about.

17

THE SECOND WEEK

Monday, May 19th –The beginning of our second week in California. Lawr flew into Oakland on an early flight, so Joan and I drove over to meet him at the airport. We welcomed the support. He took the Red Eye—no problem for Lawr. From babyhood on, he was always able to readily fall asleep. We left the airport and had breakfast together in a small coffee shop where we brought him up-to-date on the trial, before heading over to the courthouse. It would be Joan's last hours there.

As Joan, Lawr and I walked into the courtroom, I noticed Lawr tighten up. It would not be easy for him. He and Mary had a special relationship. With his job at Exxon, he had weeks of time off between sails, which he spent in Schenectady or at a favorite vacation spot, Lake George. Mary and he had shared that love of Lake George and the Adirondacks. Now, he was here to confront the man who took her life. As we filed into our seats, the main actors of this courtroom drama walked in. When International sat down, Lawr stared at him, his eyes burning a hole into the accused murderer.

Anderson put three Berkeley City Police officers on the stand. All had patrol beats in the area where International claimed to be in the early hours of August 16th. None remembered seeing International on the streets of Berkeley during that time. Next, a criminologist from the Alameda County Sheriff's Department detailed her findings in examining blood and other bodily fluid samples taken from Mary and Greg's bodies. It was gruesome testimony to hear, and my grief was compounded when the physical evidence taken from them was designated as "Bag #1", "Bag #2", "Bag #3", etc.

As I sat there in the courtroom, I felt as though my very soul was being assaulted. But I found strength from an unlikely source, a newspaper story in the *San Francisco Chronicle* written by Ruthe Stein, entitled, "A Last Vigil for Their Kids -Why parents attend trials of their children's killers." It appeared on May 15, 1986. We were following the local papers closely so this article had perfect timing. Several families who attended homicide trials of their loved ones revealed what helped them get through it. One mother said to keep from screaming, she bit down on Life Savers. Another parent said attending the trial gave her a sense of "completion."

The reporter questioned why parents would put themselves through such agony. The parents said their presence at the trial is the last thing they can do for their child. That was exactly my feeling now, as I recalled their stories and deepened my resolve to be there for Mary. The article was so powerful and persuasive that I often send it to grieving families who think they could never attend their loved one's trial.

The DA's next witness, Jack Richardson, a retired Oakland Police Officer and a firearms expert, described "the .44 Magnum as the most powerful pistol cartridge ever produced." In his testimony, he differentiated between bullets fired from rifles and those fired from revolvers.

> *The muzzle velocity of a .44 Magnum fired from a revolver with a four-inch barrel is 1,180 feet per second and its muzzle energy is 741 pounds. When the same cartridge is fired in a rifle, the bullets muzzle velocity increases to 1,750 feet per second and its muzzle energy to 1630 pounds. The reason for this increase is that the bullet, while traveling the greater length of a rifle's barrel, has more time to absorb energy from the gunpowder that is ignited when the weapon is fired.*

As a homicide inspector, Richardson had attended several hundred autopsies to study knife and bullet wounds and he had never seen a handgun cause an exit wound as massive as the one he saw in Mary. He concluded this amount of damage would be normal for a high-powered rifle.

This was particularly difficult testimony for us to hear. I could feel both Joan and Lawr stiffen when they heard about the extensive wounds that Mary and Greg had suffered. I bit my lips, closed my eyes, and prayed to Mary for the courage to sit there and not scream.

The Public Defender in cross-examining Richardson sought to establish that the rifle used in these murders could have been one that is used to shoot deer, not necessarily the rifle that International claimed was stolen.

During the trial, I saw a substitute rifle, similar to the missing one, standing in the entrance to the courtroom. I questioned a guard about it. When he said, "That's a .44 magnum rifle," I trembled as I thought, *My God, was this what killed our kids!* It was displayed in the courtroom so that the jurors could see the magnitude of a .44 magnum rifle.

After Richardson's testimony, court adjourned until the afternoon. Lawr and I drove Joan to the airport for her flight home. She hated to leave before the defense put on its witnesses but she had been away from home for over a week. At the airport, when her plane was delayed, she became worried that she might not reach her husband, Mike, and Dan to let them know she would arrive later than scheduled. They were to go to a Yankee game before heading to the airport to pick her up. Her journal entry doesn't mention who the Yankees played that day. If it were the Boston Red Sox, there might have been trouble as Mike is a dyed-in-the-wool Red Sox fan, while Dan is solidly for the Yankees. It must have turned out satisfactorily, as Joan was picked up when her plane finally landed in Newark.

While Joan waited to board the plane at San Francisco, she summarized her feelings on the last few days in her journal:

> *I took notes the whole trial. Just hope International gets convicted. Don't know how we'll feel otherwise! Justice must be served – for Mary and Greg's sakes.I am glad I came out here. I was really tired some nights, but I have felt the baby moving and have not felt sick in any way since I've been here in California, which is nice but under*

these circumstances, it's hard to really appreciate it.

I cried at different times with Mom out here, but never really broke down completely. I guess I didn't want to upset her or myself more. We have been told by a number of people that it is very hard to decide a case on purely circumstantial evidence—but that's all we have here.

International had a record—12 previous convictions—of which the jury cannot know about unless he is convicted—or unless he is put on the stand. Then, they can bring up one of his previous convictions. Big deal! He was obviously a sexual pervert, angered at times, and violent at times. He owned a rifle which disappeared that night He was the last person seen with Mary and Greg, his corn-cob pipe was found at the scene. He identified Mary in the water. But no bloody clothes or gun has been found. He has fishy alibis for what he did all night long—walking approximately 18 miles to get beer, get dope, and do his laundry!

It's too bad Mary and Greg happened to be there that night. Mary should be alive and living it up out west here if that's what she wanted! My doubt is gone from my mind—and hope—that it possibly wasn't her. But I am glad I never saw her or the pictures of her afterwards. I almost saw one of the pictures accidentally when one of the witnesses flashed it up on the stand, but I turned away. I never want to have that picture of her in my mind. I always want to remember her as the fun-loving person and good sister she was and always will be to me. I will see her and Dad in heaven one day – I pray for that.

After leaving Joan at the airport, Lawr and I headed back for the afternoon court session. Before the jury came back, a discussion centered on what would be allowed in as evidence. Anderson argued that notebooks and papers containing numerous references to firearms found in International's car should be shown to the jury to demonstrate his preoccupation with weapons. The Judge ruled they could be introduced but Anderson's request that the jury hear that the witness, Lenise (Chris) Allen, left Rainbow Village on the 15th to surrender to traffic warrants could not, as it might prejudice against the witness.

When the jury returned, the trial continued. The next witness was Lenise (Chris) Allen, International's girlfriend, who shared rental space with him for her 1967 Datsun. Anderson asked her if she left the Village on personal business. She said yes, she was away 23 days but Detectives Wolke and Eihl contacted her asking permission to search her car. Anderson showed her a paper with her signature and International's, the date, August 14th. It was the paper turning the .44 magnum rifle over to him after he paid off a debt, she said.

Public Defender Chaffee questioned Chris whether she knew the witnesses from Rainbow Village that had already testified. She said she did. When asked if she met Mary and Greg, she said yes. He questioned her also about leaving the Village on August 15th. She said she left at 11:45 am. When she said goodbye to International, he did not seem upset. Chris admitted she met another one of the witnesses, Vivian Cercey, several times over the last six months, usually talking about Cercey's children. When asked if International owned camouflage pants, she said yes, she got them at the Berkeley Free Box. And when questioned if she ever walked with Thomas up to town, she responded, "Just about every morning."

Chaffee now, through his questioning, drew the scenario of the purchase of the rifle. He showed a bill of sale, dated April 23, 1985, from Martin Barbena to Chris. She explained she went to Barbena's home with International and Bill Corruthers, as both had expressed interest in the rifle. Since neither one had a valid I.D., she signed the bill of sale. The rifle remained in her and International's possession at Rainbow Village during the summer of '85. In the questioning, Chris said she never paid any money to Barbena for the gun and responded "yes," when asked if International had a child with Barbena's sister. When Chris left the stand, she was subject to recall.

Next, Inspector Wolke was brought back to the stand to repeat what he said about International's visit to the police station on August 20th when he reported the stolen rifle. Wolke said International described it, gave the serial number, and said he purchased it from a white male, Bill, at Telegraph & Durant, for $125. I immediately noted how this was a much different scenario than what Chris had just testified as to how the rifle was purchased.

Wolke then repeated International's long account of his whereabouts during the night of August 15th and early morning hours of August 16th. When Wolke suggested International take a polygraph about the missing rifle, International inquired about the whereabouts of the Public Defender's Office.

Wolke also described searching International's car and parking space on August 26th, after a search warrant was obtained. A rifle case covered with blankets was found at a fence near International's car and other items belonging to a .44 magnum rifle were discovered in his car. In the glove box, there were papers about firearms, and a publication, "Tip Shooter." After the search, Wolke said he and Detective Eihl brought International to the Hall of Justice and at 5pm, he was arrested.

After Wolke finished his testimony, court adjourned for the day. Outside the courthouse, Lawr had a chance to speak with David and Dorothy. David was especially interested to learn that Lawr had just completed an MBA (Masters of Business Administration) at Columbia University as David was also employed as a financial advisor. Lawr thanked them for the loan of the VW, of which he had quickly taken over the wheel. He seemed amazed that I, his mother, had been able to handle those steep hills in Oakland! I was too.

Lawr drove back to Jean's. He was happy to see her, as he and Mary Ann had stayed with her when they were out in California on vacation last year.

18

THE SECOND WEEK CONTINUES

Tuesday, May 20th - We were back at the courthouse. Most days we made our way up to Jim Anderson's office, where he discussed the case with us—what had already gone on and what he hoped to present that day. It was informal but very helpful to us, members of the victims' families, to better understand the mechanics of a murder trial and the rationale of the prosecution case.

In the courtroom, Inspector Wolke was back in the witness box. The Public Defender concentrated on International's interview at the police station on August 20th when he went to report his stolen gun. While there, International was questioned by the police about the events of the night of August 15th, his several trips out of the Village to buy beer, dope, and to do his laundry. He told the police about meeting Mary and Greg along the road, smoking marijuana with them, and seeing Vince Johnson come by.

The Public Defender asked Wolke if the conversation at the police station had been taped, or written down verbatim. He said it hadn't.

Again, Wolke was asked, "Sometime after this conversation with International on the 20th, in fact on August 26, you obtained a search warrant?"

"Yes."

"You and Detective Eihl arrested him?"

"Yes."

"What time?"

"5 p.m."

Wolke said that after International was arrested, an officer was left at his car to secure the space. When the space was searched, no bloody clothing or personal items of Mary or Greg were found.

Regarding the missing rifle, the Public Defender, Chaffee, asked, "Did you search for a rifle?"

"Yes".

"Did you search the other areas around Rainbow Village?"

"Yes, we searched the entire area on many occasions. Anything we could go through, including the field by University Avenue and Marina Blvd."

"And you searched the whole area out at the marina?"

"I say as best we could because there were trucks coming in each day."

On redirect questioning, Jim Anderson asked: "Was any attempt made to search the waters?"

Wolke replied, "Not all the area. From the point up to Captain Claus' boat."

Anderson: "Water around the peninsula not searched?"

"No way to do it."

At this time, the Public Defender recalled Lenise (Chris) Allen. He asked whether International ever accompanied her to the laundry, and whether he ever went by himself. She responded he had gone with her sometimes, and if she was not feeling well, she would give him the money and he would go up to do it.

Chaffee then questioned her about when she had last seen Vivian Cercey. She said it was about the 16th of December, when Cercey was about to leave town and was trying to cash a check. She said she has not seen Cercey since and does not know where she is now.

On redirect, Anderson asked about International doing laundry and how many times he did it by himself. She answered, "Three or four times. If he doesn't have enough laundry, he does it in the sink."

Chris said she has an 11-year old son living with her, who, because he was "too long" (I assumed she meant to fit in her car) he stayed on the Blunder Bus, which Randy owned. Bill Corruthers also lived in the bus, along with anyone waiting to see a concert by the Grateful Dead.

Anderson questioned her about Vivian Cercey. Chris said she would see her parked there two or three nights a week.

"Did you ever notice her parking her car at the point?"

"Yes."

"Describe Vivian Cercey."

"In her 20's. Small build, shoulder-length, brownish color hair."

Chris did not know where Cercey lived when she was not at Rainbow Village. She said her car was a "beat-up Dodge Dart, brown."

Anderson attempted to ask Chris the following questions, but they were all objected to by the Public Defender:

"Was the defendant working when he lived at Rainbow Village? Was your son attending school in Berkeley? When was the first time your son stayed on the Blunder Bus?"

Anderson was allowed to ask: "What laundromat would you and the defendant use?"

"On San Pablo, just off University."

"Did you walk to that location?"

"Sometimes."

"How would you get there when you didn't walk?"

"I would have someone take me down there....Randy would take me there. When Mr. Thomas went with me, Mr. Thomas would help me carry the laundry."

"Did you or the defendant ever do your laundry at 6a.m. in the morning?"

"No."

With Chris Allen's testimony completed, the jury was excused for the day.

With the jury gone, Harry Shorman was now called up to the stand. A discussion followed about Vivian Cercey, who had not yet been found to bring her back to testify at the trial. Shorman said he was at his sister's house in Albany, California that morning. He thought Vivian might have called there as that was where he received telephone messages from her.

Shorman said, "I am desperately trying to reach her. Her mother is in Boston. The Welfare Department of Boston is one of the last places they have been on welfare. You could probably find her address from her mother."

Jim Anderson tried to argue that Chaffee had not used due diligence to find Cercey. However, the Judge allowed additional time to trace her.

Judge Byers rejected Chaffee's motion for a mistrial, concluding there was sufficient circumstantial evidence to continue but he would consider a second motion to reduce the charges. The Judge postponed defense testimony for another day, ordering Chaffee to make another effort to locate his "star witness," Vivian Cercey. The Judge also said he would rule on the admissibility of Chaffee reading the transcript of testimony Cercey gave at the preliminary hearing to the jury if she could not be located.

> *After only four days of testimony, the prosecution rested its case yesterday....Defense attorney Jim Chaffee promptly requested a mistrial, saying the prosecution had failed to produce evidence indicating Thomas' guilt beyond a reasonable doubt....Cercey's former lover, Harry Shorman, testified that he had recently received several telephone messages from Cercey, saying she had given birth to Shorman's child, and giving a return number in Wisconsin.*
>
> *J.E. Cooper, DA rests case in Rainbow Village trial.* Daily Californian, *May 21, 1986.*

That night, the three of us met Jean's daughter, Diana, in Berkeley. Lawr met Diana a few years before when working for Exxon, and his ship would moor in San Francisco Bay. While there, he would often catch up with Jean and Diana. Tonight we had dinner together in one of Berkeley's unique restaurants, which Diana chose.

We strolled around briefly beforehand, checking some of the store windows, stocked with psychedelic merchandise. Young people, many of them students from the University of California at Berkeley, milled around the coffee shops and bookstores. Mary would have liked this place with its history of a strong social conscience and a somewhat "hippie" atmosphere.

At dinner, Lawr ordered an entree served with rice that looked half white, half dark (probably brown natural rice). He said, "This looks like rice that can't make up its mind!" The little things that made us laugh at a time when we thought we could never laugh again gave a glimpse that healing was possible.

Wednesday, May 21st – Today was an off-day, with no court session scheduled until tomorrow. Lawr had an idea. I'm sure he thought it would help raise my spirits.

"Let's take a drive up to Napa Valley and see some of the wine country. Mary Ann and I were there last year. It was great. It'll give us a break from all that courtroom stuff."

"Sounds good," I said. It would be a welcome retreat from having to think about courtrooms, witnesses and especially Ralph International Thomas, for one day.

After breakfast, we left the Oakland hills and headed north. Lawr also wanted to show me where his ship docked when it arrived at San Francisco headed for Canada along the coastline. After seeing this, we took a side trip over to Benicia, one of California's most historic small towns. When California was only a territory, it had been the state capital for a short time.

"I think you'll like this town; it's real picturesque," Lawr told me.

He was right, and there was lots of information there about California, which I was slowly digesting. Leaving Benicia, we made our way over to Route 29, the trail that runs north through the wine country. We stopped at several of the wineries and took short, but informative, tours of their facilities. What a great way to learn more about wine-making. Of course, at the end of each tour, the wine tasting was an added treat.

The Robert Mondavi Winery had buildings that resembled an old southwestern mission. I looked around for the monks, but saw none. We made certain to stop at the Inglenook Winery, as Jean had once designed some of their labels.

After an early dinner at one of the fine restaurants in Napa, we headed back to our "home away from home" in Oakland and shared our adventures with Jean.

Thursday, May 22nd. In the morning, Lawr and I drove to the Oakland Courthouse. Yesterday had been a good break from the trial.

As we entered the courtroom, a discussion about finding

Vivian Cercey, the defense's key witness, took place before the jury was seated. Chaffee said Harry Shorman's sister told him Vivian had a baby girl born two weeks earlier on May 12. Chaffee again repeated all the steps taken to reach her. Jim Anderson retorted that the defense knew back in March that Cercey would be a material witness and had waited until now for Harry Shorman to give them this information. Anderson said, "Now Vivian is the center of attention, everyone scurrying around. Before, no one attempted to locate her." He asked Judge Byers not to allow her former testimony to be read at the trial. The Judge responded that Cercey should be present but will allow the defense until next week to find her. The jury then was called into the courtroom.

Martin Barbena, the first defense witness, said he knew the defendant because International had lived with his sister for several years, and they had a child. Barbena testified he wanted to sell the rifle, and that title was transferred to Lenise Allen, International's girlfriend, because she had valid identification.

Anderson, in his cross-examination, emphasized that International had access to the rifle even if Barbena sold it to Lenise. Barbena described the rifle as a bolt action Remington Model 788 with its box magazine missing and the breech recessed. To load it, the cartridge had to be inserted in the chamber by hand to prevent jamming. With probing by Anderson, Barbena conceded that in order to fire a second shot, the rifle had to be reloaded very carefully.

Chaffee recalled Tracy Scarborough, the man who slept in International's car the night of the murders, asking about his use of alcohol and whether he had an alcohol problem. Tracy admitted, "Yes, had it about eight years," and that sometimes he is unable to remember things and has blackouts.

Next, an air traffic controller from the Oakland airport testified about weather conditions on August 16th. It was overcast, 10 miles visibility, with no moon visible. To this, Anderson added, "No celestial bodies that night could be seen."

Judge Byers then excused the jury until Tuesday, granting the defense Friday and the weekend to find Cercey. Monday was the Memorial Day Holiday.

We were back in the courtroom after lunch without the jury. Chaffee pushed to have the charges lowered to second degree murder. The discussion that followed detailed the difference between first degree and second degree murder. It is determined by how intent was formed. Pre-meditated first degree is established only when a killing is the result of careful thought and planning. Chaffee argued that this case did not show that the killings were the result of careful thought and were not pre-conceived.

Anderson picked up on the planning element, recalling that International was down on the road, passed by Mary and Greg, and smoked a joint. Anderson continued, "Somehow that gun had to get from his vehicle to the access road. That gun had to be brought down there with a specific purpose. If you bring a gun 125 yards somewhere, there is sufficient planning on somebody's part." He cited the forensic pathologist's description of the injuries incurred on the victims before death and also that the butt of the rifle was used on Mary. Anderson said the manner of killing - press contact wounds - was not accidental.

Once more, it was so hard to sit there and hear what happened to Mary and Greg. Lawr sat next to me, and I could feel him tighten up as he listened.

The Judge, now off the record, gave his view of the case. He stated that there was no way that one murder was not pre-meditated. The weapon was moved from the car; it was not semi-automatic and required a bolt action - it had to be pulled back. He said the law does not require a specific time for pre-meditation. "I think there is more than sufficient evidence to go to the jury on that question."

A charge of manslaughter was discussed, but the Judge said he would reserve ruling on manslaughter until both sides rested. He wanted to review the cases that the defense cited.

When this discussion ended, Lawr said goodbye to Jim Anderson and thanked him for his strong pursuit of justice for Mary and Greg. "I hate to leave before it's over but I have to get back." Turning to David and Dorothy, he said, "I know it's been hard for all of us, having to sit here and listen to this, but, again, I really believe that by our being here, Greg and Mary are here too."

The next day Jean and I took him to the airport. We

hugged and said our farewells. Lawr looked at me, saying, "I hate to leave, Mom, but I know Chris and Pat will be here in a few days for you. Love you!" After he was gone, I thought about Gerry, Lawr, and Joan, who had already been out here, and Chris and Pat, who would come next week. I knew I was very fortunate to have the love and support of all of them. We had always been close but Mary's death made the family circle even tighter.

Jean had the weekend off because it was the Memorial Day holiday. On Saturday, we did some touring. Because of our many conversations, Jean knew I wanted to see some of the places Mary wrote about, especially Santa Cruz. Her envelope was addressed, "Long Lost Mary, Santa Cruz, CA," and mailed from Oakland.

We left Jean's in the late morning and drove south to the San Mateo Bridge, which stretches across the southern section of San Francisco Bay. Jean lived in California for many years and was an excellent tour guide. She noted points of interest as we drove. We went through San Jose but didn't stop. Our final destination was Santa Cruz, with Monterey Bay to the west and shelved in by the Santa Cruz mountains to the east. Along the way, we stopped briefly to look at the impressive coastline. I remembered Mary wrote, *At my friend Rusty's near the ocean in Santa Cruz, not too far anyway. If I listen for it I hear the waves crashing in.*

We stopped for a short time at a small café overlooking the ocean. As we sat there, sipping our coffee, I wondered if it was the one Mary was at when she wrote, *Right now I am sitting in a coffee shop in Santa Cruz sipping some coffee....*

Young people wandered about in the coffee shop and down by the bay. Most were probably students from the University of California at Santa Cruz. Its large, impressive campus was nearby, built into the mountains. After viewing the University, Jean headed further up the mountain road. We knew we wouldn't find it but we had to look:

> I must meet a friend of mine soon; she has
> some of my things. They live in a house up on the
> mountains above Santa Cruz and they have one of
> my knapsacks up there for storage. She is coming

155

*into town today so I called her and asked if she
would bring me some things.*

I could never thank Jean enough for the patience and
kindness she showed me during those incredibly tough days in
California. She assisted in my desperate search for Mary and my
attempt to walk where she walked in her last days of life, so very
far from home. Jean had three daughters and said she could only
imagine the agony that a parent of a murdered child must
endure.

Sunday night found us at Jean's Singles Club mixer. She
did her best to see that I had some fun and diversion mixed in
my California experience. We drove down to the local church
where the group met in a large hall. Some members asked what
I was doing in California and I answered I wanted to see the
other half of the country. No need to go deeper. Who would ever
guess or want to hear that I was out here to attend the trial of my
daughter's murderer?

Later some of Jean's friends decided to go out to a nearby club. We gathered around the piano for an old-fashioned sing-
along. When strains of Frank Sinatra's "New York, New York"
began, tears streamed down my face, and I sang the words with
fervor. After two weeks in California, I realized I was homesick.

19

THE THIRD AND FINAL WEEK

Tuesday, May 27th - The long weekend was over. I found myself back at the Alameda courthouse, this time alone. Lawr had returned home and Chris and Patrick would arrive tonight. When I reached there, David and Dorothy were already in Jim Anderson's office. He was angry because Vivian Cercey was still missing and her testimony would have to be read to the jury. After listening to Jim's tirade, we proceeded downstairs to the courtroom and filed into our usual front row seats.

The Public Defender called the first witness - an investigator from his office, who described his efforts to find Cercey. Chaffee said he had tried to locate her last December but no one knew where she went; she didn't take her car.

Jim Anderson argued that due diligence had not been used to find Cercey. The Judge disagreed, saying both Harry Shorman and Vivian Cercey were "floaters," so subpoenas could not be issued when her whereabouts were unknown. The Judge announced he would allow Cercey's previous testimony - 86 pages in total - to be read in her absence. And he will read it to the jury. I am sure the defense would have preferred Susan Walsh, Chaffee's assistant, do the reading. Having a woman read the testimony may have sounded better and might even help their case.

As the trial progressed, I became upset, even angry, to see Walsh sit next to International. She occasionally offered him gum or candy, smiled at him, appearing ultra-friendly. I thought,

How can she do that? I know she is his defense attorney and cannot treat him as a pariah, even though I would! Again it may be a play to the jury to see a woman sit near him, calmly, not at all frightened.

After this announcement about the reading, the jury was dismissed until 1:30pm, when they would be back to listen to Cercey's testimony.

Now Cercey's statement was gone over thoroughly. Jim Anderson, Susan Walsh for the Public Defender, and the Judge worked on this, making several changes. With Cercey absent, any objections to the statement had to be addressed before it was presented to the jury. Once the testimony was agreed to, it was filed with the court, and ready for the Judge to read.

At lunchtime, David, Dorothy and I discussed this latest development.

"Do you think Cercey really couldn't be found?" I asked David, skeptically.

"I think they're conveniently keeping her away from the courtroom to make their case better, if that's possible," David responded.

"Well, I'm glad Judge Byers didn't allow Susan Walsh to read it. The Judge's reading will be 'non-partisan,' if we can use that expression in a trial."

Back in the courtroom after lunch, the Judge addressed the jury and explained that since Cercey was unavailable, his reading of her testimony should be considered as if she were on the stand – "like any other witness." This reading would not be recorded by the stenotypist; instead, a corrected copy of her testimony would be inserted into the trial record.

Then Judge Byers began: "Berkeley Municipal Court, November 7, 1985, Preliminary Hearing….." He continued reading until the testimony was complete.

Immediately following, Anderson recalled Inspector Dan Wolke to the stand, questioning him about Vivian Cercey. Wolke said he interviewed her on August 17, about 2:15 – 2:30pm, after the second body was found. At the time, she was outside the gate at Rainbow Village and Harry Shorman introduced her to him. Wolke described the interview and pointed out inconsistencies in what she told him at that time when compared to her later story.

Next, Anderson recalled Vincent Johnson. Anderson asked him if he knew Vivian Cercey. "Yes, she had a relationship with Harry Shorman." Then Johnson continued and told how he was in Berkeley last Friday and read that day's issue of <u>The Daily Californian.</u>

Anderson: "After reading an article in <u>The Daily Californian</u> about a witness being sought, did you go to the Berkeley Police Department and indicate certain things about what you read in the paper?"

Johnson answered, "Yes."

Anderson continued, "Back in September or October, when you saw Vivian Cercey at Rainbow Village, did you discuss the events of August 16 and August 17?"

Johnson: "Yes, she told me, basically, that everything she said she was told to say by Harry Shorman and, basically, had not seen anything."

Anderson: "And when you saw that article in the paper, did that prompt you to go to Inspector Wolke, and did you tell him what you told us today?"

Johnson: "Yes."

The Public Defender then questioned Johnson about when and where his conversation with Cercey took place.

"In front of Harry Shorman's bus, about 15 to 20 feet in front of the door."

"What time of day?"

"Maybe about 2 to 3pm.

"Do you know this for a fact?"

"Just estimating."

"Anyone else there?"

"No."

Chaffee asked if Cercey's kids were with her at the time. Johnson said she was carrying her smallest kid in her arm. "How long did the conversation last?"

"About three to four minutes."

"You started asking her questions about what she had seen last August?"

"Yes."

"And she said, 'just made it up.' Harry made her?"

"Everything she said, Harry told her to say it. She said she was speaking about it because Harry told her to. She said she really didn't see anything that night."

When this surprising testimony concluded, recess was called until the next morning when summations by both sides would be heard. With the jury dispersed, Judge Byers told Anderson and Chaffee that he reviewed the cases they had submitted to him and decided that the charge could not be reduced to voluntary manslaughter.

We left the courthouse, free until closing arguments the next day.

That night, Jean and I went to the Oakland airport to pick up Christine and Patrick. They left Boston at 7pm and arrived at midnight. I was anxious to see them. I had kept in close touch with the family during the time I was out in California but there is nothing like having a family member right there beside you as you go through something like this.

It was their first trip to California so they were excited even if the nature of their trip was not particularly happy. After hugs and kisses, and introducing them to Jean, we headed back to her house. I filled them in on what had happened at the trial thus far and the surprising testimony of Vince Johnson today. We all believed International was guilty but Johnson's testimony showed the weakness of the defense case with their prime witness now exposed.

It was late; we needed to get Chris and Patrick settled in their new quarters. Jean's house turned into a Gioia boarding house in those days and weeks. Now everyone needed to get some sleep to be prepared for the next day.

Wednesday, May 28th – This was a critical day for us. All the witnesses had been heard, even one by proxy. It was now up to the two attorneys - Jim Anderson and Jim Chaffee - to present their final arguments to the jury. I was nervous. The jury would now consider all the evidence presented by the prosecution, which I firmly believed showed International's guilt. On the other hand, Chaffee, the Public Defender, would also lay all his cards of doubt on the table.

We arrived at the courthouse and headed up to Jim Anderson's office. Today there were two more members of the family for him to meet. David and Dorothy were already there.By this time, they heard a lot about all of the Gioia's so they were happy to meet two more. Following introductions and a short briefing by Jim Anderson, we took the elevator down to the all too familiar courtroom. I showed Chris and Pat where we usually sat. After we were seated, the closing arguments began.

Jim Anderson led off, saying, "Whenever attorneys address you by way of closing arguments, what we say is not evidence. We are only advocates. I will be arguing from my point of view and Chaffee from his point of view."

Anderson then requested the horrific pictures of Mary and Greg, as they were found in the waters, to be put up on the board, once again for the jury to see what had happened to them. I warned Chris and Pat this might occur so we developed a plan. While these photos were shown on the screen, we three kept our eyes lowered, looking at a small photo of Mary I held on my lap. None of us wanted these terrible images of her burned in our minds forever.

Anderson continued to argue hard, referring to International as a "modern day Rainbow Village Rambo."

> *Anderson began his closing arguments by stressing the weight of circumstantial evidence against Thomas. Thomas owned a Remington .44 magnum rifle, and both victims had been shot with a large caliber rifle...Anderson charged that Thomas wanted to molest Gioia, and displayed a photo of Gioia's unbuttoned, unzippered culottes as found on her body. Gioia's resistance and Kniffin's defense led to their deaths, Anderson speculated....*
>
> *J.E. Cooper. Jury deliberates Rainbow Village case.* <u>The Daily Californian</u>, *May 30, 1986.*

It also noted that Anderson disputed International's alibi that he walked back and forth to Berkeley several times when the murders occurred. "Fifteen miles – that's an amazing performance after drinking liquor and smoking dope and no sleep," was how Anderson described it.

The DA also argued the other inconsistencies International told the police. First, that Mary had called him over to ask for a match, when two waterlogged matchbooks were found on her body. Next, that his gun and ammunition had been stolen, although he asked a neighbor to "hide his ammo." And, finally, that he told a neighbor he was "dumpster diving" when the murders occurred.

The Public Defender, Chaffee, began his remarks, "Don't want to argue – want to talk." As I heard him speak and observed his mannerisms, he very much reminded me of the actor, Vincent Price, who I had seen on the screen many years ago. Chaffee contrasted Anderson and spoke in a soft, almost subdued, manner. He spoke so low that the stenotypist asked to move closer to him so that she could record his remarks.

Again, <u>The Daily Californian</u>:

> *Public Defender Jim Chaffee challenged Anderson's inferences of Thomas' guilt from circumstantial evidence, and called most of Anderson's points "trivial" and "exaggerated." Chaffee began his remarks with what he called the "simple arithmetic" of Thomas' total walking mileage before daybreak, which Chaffee calculated to be 13.2 miles. "Assuming he was sauntering, walking at the rate of three and a half miles per hour, there was plenty of time available to walk the distance."*

Chaffee pointed out also that his star witness, Vivian Cercey's testimony was corroborated by a photo that showed two liquor bottles found in the Village dumpster, where she said she saw the murder victims argue with a "blond man" that night. "This photo is a marker of (Cercey's) honor, her veracity." And Chaffee rejected Vincent Johnson's testimony that Cercey told him she had not seen anything and was told what to say by Harry Shorman. Chaffee said Johnson and Thomas "never got along."

<u>The Daily Californian</u> article concluded,

> *Anderson focused his rebuttal of Chaffee's remarks with attacks on both Thomas' and Cercey's statements. Calling Thomas' credibility "next to zero," Anderson said the lack of physical evidence in the case resulted from Thomas' attempts to cover his tracks before his arrest on August 26. Anderson cited inconsistencies in Cercey's testimony, includ-*

ing her descriptions of the victims and of the weather, and said her account was "ludicrous at best, perjurious at worst."

When the closing remarks were over, we left the courtroom and spoke briefly to David and Dorothy. It had been a very emotional day for all of us. How many times can we listen to the terrible fate that happened to our kids! But we would be back the next day. The jury would get its instructions and prepare to deliberate Ralph International Thomas' fate.

When we left the courthouse, Chris and Pat wanted to see Rainbow Village. It would be difficult for them to see where Chris' little birthday sister and Patrick's next-down-the-line sibling met her death. Patrick was now at the wheel of the VW bug. We drove over to Berkeley and soon reached the site of Rainbow Village.

We crossed over the strip of land to where the Village had been and I directed Patrick past Claus von Wendel's boat, still awaiting the start of its long voyage. We drove slowly along the inlet shore next to the rocks. I pointed out the spot where I believed Mary and Greg had sat looking over at the hills of Berkeley. We stopped and got out of the car.

"I think this is where it happened," I said, my voice shaking. I was well aware how difficult it was for these two to contemplate all of what had gone on at that very site. We held hands and quietly whispered a prayer to our Mary.

We headed up the road from the shore to where the Village had once been. Christine had a camera and said, "I want to take some photos of this place, although I know how hard it will always be to look at them."

One of the buses was still parked there behind the fence. We saw no one; it looked completely deserted. It was hard to imagine that there was life and activity going on there just a year before. Chris took a few more pictures of the closed-up Village, very aware that this is where Mary had spent her last hours on this earth.

When our emotional pilgrimage was finished, we drove back to Jean's. It was a beautiful California day so the three of us headed out for a walk. With the entrance to the Redwood Regional Park close by, almost directly behind Jean's house, we

163

strolled along the path, the tall redwood trees shading us from the afternoon sun. We marveled at the magnificence of nature, trying to imagine how many years these trees had been here, in this very spot. Patrick, one of a few avid campers in our family, commented, "I think this could give the Adirondacks a run for its money." Laughing, I said, "Where's your New York spirit—but I think you could be right."

Despite the compelling beauty of the place, it was difficult to put the trial out of our minds. As we walked, Chris and Pat had questions about what had taken place before they arrived. I reviewed each day and gave them a synopsis of all the characters that were witnesses for both sides. They were familiar with much of it because yesterday's closing arguments had been a good review.

Thursday, May 29th - The three of us arrived at the courthouse. It would be my last day out here. I had a plane reservation to leave that afternoon. We filed into our usual front row seats, David and Dorothy already there.

I felt apprehensive and nervous. The District Attorney, Jim Anderson, had presented very strong arguments for what had happened to Mary and Greg and, in my opinion, painted a clear picture proving International's guilt. I realized though that I am so close to this and naturally would be biased. Will the jurors— these twelve people I have seen each day sitting in that jury box—come to the same conclusion? Some days, as I rode the elevator in the courthouse, I would spot one or two of them, almost next to me. I was careful to not lock eyes with them as they would clearly see my pain. I realized one is not to have any contact with the jurors during the trial.

As the jurors took their seats, I wondered if they were relieved that the trial was almost over. Their lives would soon return to normal. Would ours? The familiar, "All rise" was called out as Judge Byers entered from his chambers and sat down. He looked directly at the jury and began to read their instructions "that the law requires you to follow." I was nervous, but wrote a few down.

Apply law to the facts as you determine and

164

arrive at a verdict.

> *You must not be influenced by pity or bias.*
>
> *You must not infer that he is more likely to be guilty than innocent.*
>
> *Statements made by attorneys during the trial are not evidence.*
>
> *A question is not evidence.*

As the long list of instructions was read, I listened intently, staring at the jurors trying to read their expressions but surmised nothing from this exercise. The Judge continued:

> *You must not draw any inference if defendant does not testify.*

Jim Anderson had mentioned to us that there was a pre-agreement—between the Judge, Chaffee and himself—that if International took the stand in his own defense, one of his prior charges could be raised by Anderson. He probably would have questioned International about one of his previous rapes, as he believed rape or sexual assault was a prime motive in our case.

A few others I wrote down:

> *Specific intent must exist.*
>
> *Defendant has introduced evidence to prove he was not there at the time of the crime. If you feel all the evidence shows he was not there, you must acquit him.*

Judge Byers told the jurors they had to agree unanimously whether International was guilty or not guilty. They had to agree whether the murders were first degree or second degree. Since the defendant was charged with the use of a firearm in the commission of the crime, if they determined that he did use one, that finding would be a felony. Another proviso was that if the defendant was convicted of more than one murder, and one was first degree, special circumstances must be proved beyond a reasonable doubt.

At the conclusion of all the instructions, Judge Byers left the courtroom. The jury, still appearing deadpan to me, then filed out to begin their awesome task. After listening to all the days of testimony, I wondered what they would conclude. Will they find

International guilty or innocent? I know I will never be permitted to serve on a criminal jury, at least not one that is to decide a murder case. When a loved one is violently murdered, your perspective on life and what is important drastically changes. I will always look through dark glasses at anyone who commits a crime, especially murder. But it is not for me to decide on this crime, this murder.

As I left the courtroom that day, I wondered if this would be the last time I would see this place. If the jurors were unanimous in finding International guilty, I would be back.

All of us had lunch together one last time. Later, I headed over to San Francisco to fly back to New York. During the flight, after almost three weeks in California, my mind was filled with everything that had gone on at the trial. It was hard to unwind. Mary continually popped into my mind. At first, happy and carefree, as I had last seen her, but then I fought back the other image, the way she was when she was found in the waters. Although I never saw her destroyed body, having listened to the trial testimony, my mind conjured up a terrible picture that over the years I would desperately try to erase.

Chris and Pat stayed in California until the next Monday, June 2nd. When they made plane reservations, they had no idea how long the trial would run. Now, they took the time they had left to explore Oakland, Berkeley, and San Francisco. They remained at Jean's and had the use of the VW bug until they left for home. When they returned, they had some great stories to tell about their adventures. In San Francisco, they rode the cable car and hung out at Fisherman's Wharf with thousands of other visitors to this exciting city. They visited Haight Asbury and the Fillmore Auditorium, where the Grateful Dead played, and listened to the music of the street players. And they lit up when they described driving down Lombard Street, "the crookedest street in the world," in that little VW, at the speed limit of 5 miles per hour!

20

BACK HOME AFTER THE TRIAL

When I landed in Newark, Dan was there to give me a ride home. As we drove up to Schenectady, my mind was filled with the last three weeks of the trial. Dan, noticeably quiet, asked a few questions about what went on, but he was not overly curious. It was still very difficult for him to hear the details of what had happened to his sister, as it only increased his anger.

All of us deal with anger in our own way, in our own time. Mary's five siblings who made the trip to California walked that last walk for her. They confronted their feelings of anger and rage each time they gazed at International as he sat right there in front of them. They represented their sister in that courtroom, showing the world that she was loved and, oh, so missed.

Dan and Robert did not attend the trial. Dan was in college and that was his place to be at that time. Mary would not have had it differently. Robert would later admit to me that he didn't go because he didn't think he could handle being in the same room with the person who murdered his sister. Both Dan and Robert have since visited Rainbow Village, when on business trips to San Francisco. In later years, we placed a plaque close to the area where Mary and Greg were murdered. They said it has helped them to stand there, think about Mary, and unburden themselves of pent-up feelings harbored all these years. Their once hot anger has been replaced by a softer feeling in their hearts, reserved for remembering and loving her.

The conversation with Dan on the ride back switched to present and mundane happenings at home, and I was brought up to date on life back on Cornelius Avenue. Away for three weeks, it was hard to put myself in this place again.

At home, when I opened my mail, I discovered a sympathy card and note from one of Mary's oldest friends, Marjorie Leary.

> *Dear Mrs. Gioia,*
>
> *I hope you don't mind me still calling you Mrs. Gioia. It's just I've always known you as that and old habits are hard to break. We've all been through much time and many changes, yet in memory the bonds we've known are still strong.*
>
> *I want to extend my love and support to you and to all your family. My thoughts and prayers continue to be with you and Mary. May your hearts and spirit be healed. I have so many memories of Mary and growing up together. Enduring clarinet lessons together, giggling till we ached, private jokes, arguments and friendly conciliation, skating nearly every day during winter at the Mohawk Club, walks home from grade school and bus rides home from high school together.*
>
> *One thing I remember most about Mary, and I'm not sure I can put it in words very well, but she had a spirit that was so encouraging to others. She was always there at school concerts that friends performed in, watching and praising and she always showed up to cheer you on at that important track meet. She didn't have to be asked; she was always there. She had a way of knowing what was important to a friend and really coming through with loving encouragement. She was open and loving and gentle in this way. This was very special about her to me.*
>
> *I know that Mary must be in some way sending that love and support to you now as you need it—maybe directly and perhaps in this way through her friends that she shared it with in her life. And so it surrounds you.*
>
> *Love, Margie*

I went back to work the next Monday, June 2nd. It was the longest stretch I had out of the office in my eight years working there. Everything ran smoothly, thanks to the staff, including Susan Troll, a Legislative Fellow assigned to us for the Session, and to Glenn von Nostitz, our Legislative Counsel. I knew Glenn from my Niskayuna political days. He and his wife, Margaret, rushed up to Schenectady from the Catskills, where they were vacationing, when they heard the news of Mary's murder. Their visit meant a lot to me, as I realized how Mary's murder affected so many more people than just our immediate family.

Everyone, including the Senator, wanted to hear about the trial so I managed a brief summation for all. Although anxious about the verdict, I found it difficult to believe International would be found innocent. However, I sensed Senator Leichter was apprehensive about the verdict. He didn't want me to harbor false expectations. But I remained firm in my belief that International would be found guilty.

On Wednesday, June 4th, I received the telephone call from Jim Anderson. I had just returned home from work and sat at the pass-through counter in the kitchen. Lawr was there too, filling me in on his graduation from Columbia Business School. It was held at the end of May and I couldn't attend because I was still out in Oakland. When the phone rang, Lawr reached over for the wall phone and answered. "Mom, it's Jim Anderson. He needs to speak to you." My body shook as I grabbed the phone. Jim's next words will always remain with me. "The jury found him guilty. So get back out here for the next trial."

Jim said the jury convicted Ralph International Thomas of first-degree murder for Greg and second degree murder for Mary, along with special circumstances related to the double homicides. The penalty phase would start next week. This same jury would decide if International should be given life without the possibility of parole or should receive a sentence of death. At the conclusion of our conversation, I told Jim I would make arrangements for a flight back to California.

When I heard, "death penalty," I had to reassess how I felt about this. I had considered myself liberal in most of my political and philosophical beliefs. It seemed only natural to be anti-death penalty. I thought then—and now—God forbid that an innocent person would be executed. Could I now accept the possibility of a death sentence in our case? When I first went out to the trial and realized that it was considered a possible death penalty case, I reserved my opinion on it. I decided I would not become embroiled in a pro- or anti-death penalty debate. Instead, I would accept whatever the jury or court decided. In 1985, California had the death penalty; New York did not. Perhaps there was room in our judicial system for the worst of the worst to receive the ultimate punishment.

The courtroom scene was described as follows when the jurors announced the verdict:

> The six-man, six-woman jury convicted Thomas of first - and second - degree murder in the August 1985 slayings of Gregory Kniffen and Mary Gioia. The prosecution charged Thomas with shooting both victims with a high-powered rifle before dumping their bodies in the bay.
>
> An impassive Thomas, dressed in jeans, plaid shirt, and the blue down jacket he has worn everyday, heard his verdict late Wednesday afternoon in a virtually empty courtroom. Parents of both victims returned to the East Coast last week.
>
> Thomas' friends and relatives, who had attended the trial since it began May 12, were not present.
>
> J.E. Cooper. Jury convicts Thomas of Rainbow Village murders. <u>The Daily Californian,</u> June 6, 1986.

The distance between California and New York made it impossible for David and me to be at the courtroom when the verdict came down. Oh, how we wanted to be there!

21

THE PENALTY PHASE BEGINS

Tuesday, June 10th – This was my third flight out to California. Although the guilty verdict is now behind us, I still feel anxious. Jean, ever the faithful friend, is there to pick me up at the San Francisco airport. After hugging me, she says, "I just knew they'd find him guilty, Pat. But now the jury has another big decision to make."

"Yeah, we're all glad they found him guilty. At least he'll spend the rest of his life in prison for what he did to Mary and Greg."

We headed back to Oakland and another restless night.

Wednesday, June 11th – In the morning I met David and Dorothy back down at the Alameda County Courthouse. David brought along a tape recorder since he learned that we could record the proceeding. I'm thankful to him for making copies of the tapes for me. They have proved invaluable as I revisited those painful days in that courtroom.

We settled into our usual seats, right near the jury box. I could feel myself tightening up as International entered the courtroom and took his seat next to the defense team. He didn't look back at us. I had to suppress crying out, *You see, you're not above the law! You will pay for what you did to Mary and Greg!*

The jurors filed in and took their seats. I looked over at them and wondered if my gratitude showed for finding this monster guilty of killing my daughter, Mary, and her friend, Greg.

They must now decide whether Ralph International Thomas will spend the rest of his life in prison, or be put to death.

Judge Byers began his detailed instructions to the jury by emphasizing a key difference between the guilt phase and this current penalty phase. In the former, the jurors were to disregard any reference to pity for the defendant, but now he explained:

> Sympathy and compassion for the defendant in this case are elements to be considered by you in the determination of his punishment. It is not only appropriate but necessary that the jury weigh the sympathetic elements of the defendant's background. The court instructs you that you may take sympathy into account in determining the appropriate penalty in this case.

I listened closely to his words and thought, where is the sympathy and compassion for Mary and Greg? I realized at that moment the criminal justice system does all it can to protect the rights of a defendant.

At last it began. I expected the Public Defender, Chaffee, to begin so I was surprised when the defense co-counsel, Susan Walsh, rose to give the defense's opening statement. I surmised another tactical decision was made to appeal to the jury: A woman will speak on behalf of this man convicted of double murder.

Walsh explained the penalty phase to the jury. "Neither side bears the burden of proof." In the guilt phase, the prosecution bore the burden of guilt. "Now, it is a weighing process," Walsh explained, and then reviewed the difference between aggravating and mitigating circumstances.

> Aggravating circumstances are bad acts, bad things that the defendant has done in his life which you may consider in making your verdict. Mitigating circumstances are good things; good things about the defendant, his character, his background, his family life, situations about him that you may consider as something that would tend to make you feel better about the defendant.

Walsh reminded them that they may consider sympathy, compassion, and empathy when deciding on a verdict. She told the jury the fact that the defendant will not testify must not be held against him. She explained that he has a constitutional right to take the stand and he will not exercise that right in this trial.

My thoughts: *Here we go again! Defendants have rights in the U.S. Constitution; victims do not.*

Walsh then released the firebomb.

> *Now I am going to talk to you about factors that do apply, of which there are four basically that apply as I see it. The first is the presence or absence of prior felony convictions.*
>
> *The defendant has suffered twelve convictions; arising out of four incidents that occurred in 1973. There were nine counts that came out of Alameda County and three counts that came out of Monterey County. He was convicted of four counts of rape, three counts of robbery, two counts of kidnapping, two counts of oral copulation and one count of sodomy.*
>
> *For these crimes, the defendant served nine years in state prison.... He served one year on parole and was released from (sic) parole on November 1, 1984.*

Walsh stated this litany of prior crimes in a very matter-of-fact manner. She might have been reading from a grocery list or reciting ingredients for a recipe. My eyes remain glued on the jury. They seemed startled, shocked. These were the "bad acts" this defendant committed.

Next, Walsh prepared the way for later testimony by three correctional officers who detailed incidents "Mr. Thomas" (she always referred to him this way) committed while in prison. She reminded them that they must accept, beyond a reasonable doubt, that a crime was committed in each instance.

> *You will also be hearing information regarding extenuating circumstances and abstracts*

of the defendant's character and background that he
may wish to offer, which may be by way of family
and friends.

Finally you will be hearing evidence of the
circumstances surrounding this crime itself.

Walsh then told the jurors Vivian Cercey will appear today in person. Previously they heard her testimony read by the Judge but she has returned to the area.

We are going to present Vivian to you today,
to allow you to judge her credibility, her demeanor,
which is something you were not able to do....

Walsh ended with the following caution:

The death penalty is never an absolute. You
always have discretion, considering whatever fac-
tors you wish to consider, including sympathy,
including compassion, and including empathy.
Remember the instructions the Judge gives you and
apply the facts to the law.

As Walsh took her seat, I wondered what was going through the minds of each of the jurors. Has Walsh prepared them to keep their minds open, to listen to the evidence, and separate the good acts from the bad? I looked over at Jim Anderson who now rose to begin his opening statement. As always, confident, self-assured, he presented his case clearly to the jury.

As Ms. Walsh indicated to you, you are now
starting the second phase of this particular trial,
and the reason why we are starting the second phase
of the trial is that you have found the defendant
guilty of two murders, one of them being in the first
degree...and the other in the second degree.

Anderson said the prosecution evidence will show that aggravating factors far outweigh the mitigating ones. Three correctional officers will appear to tell of International's altercations at three separate times while in San Quentin Prison.

Next, Anderson told the jury he will speak about International's previous crimes.

> I will introduce the certified abstracts of the defendant's prior reprehensible conduct—I don't know of any other terminology that could be used for it. We will show you that in 1974 he was convicted in Monterey County by pleading guilty to two counts of rape of females and one count of robbery.
>
> Later on, I will be introducing to you certified abstracts of a judgment that in Alameda County on November 1, 1974, he stood convicted by a jury of Alameda County citizens, not unlike you, who found him guilty of some of the most heinous crimes. Those include two counts of rape, two counts of kidnapping, two counts of forcible oral copulation, two counts of robbery and one count of sodomy, all while the defendant was armed with a handgun during the commission of those offenses.

(Anderson had told David and me he wanted some of these victims to testify at this trial but they were unwilling to do so. They did not want to be in the same room to face the man who committed such terrible crimes on them.)

Anderson further explained to the jury that the two counts of murder they already found International guilty of would be aggravating factors enough, even without the others, to warrant a prosecutor to ask them to consider a verdict of death. And that is what he will do - ask them to bring back a sentence of death. Jim took his seat. I am biased, of course, but I felt Jim presented a very strong case.

The Judge called a brief recess and excused the jurors, reminding them not to talk about the case prior to commencing deliberations.

Jim Anderson now voiced strong opposition to calling Vivian Cercey to the stand. "They are recalling her to recite her testimony, not to recant, but to give it again, for no apparent reason obviously, but to prey upon the sympathy the jury has about any lingering doubt they may have about the defendant."

Anderson argued that it is "untimely" and offered nothing because the jury already had all the evidence before them in the guilt phase. It appealed for sympathy for Cercey because she had her baby on the road and had a long trip to get back to California.

Chaffee rebutted, saying this jury never had the opportunity to "see her, hear her, watch her manner."

Despite more discussion between Anderson, Chaffee, and Judge Byers, Cercey will be allowed to give testimony in the afternoon, after recess.

After recess, discussion continued about Cercey's appearance. Jim Anderson, still adamantly opposed, argued that the defense wanted to create lingering doubt. Judge Byers told him, "Lingering doubt is still the law of the State" and repeating her testimony will allow the jury to see how she acts on the stand. The Judge then warned Chaffee that if he placed her on the stand and asked the jury to reevaluate her testimony, the District Attorney could also present evidence to help the jury reevaluate as well. With the matter settled, the jury was recalled.

Chaffee called Vivian Cercey to the witness stand. After she was sworn in, he began: "Ms. Cercey. Take a deep breath. Relax."

Cercey's testimony at this time was essentially what she said at the Preliminary Hearing. She insisted she was not intoxicated; she drank no more than four or five beers during the afternoon and evening of the 15th. She denied telling Vincent Johnson that she had not seen anything on the night of the murders.

DA Jim Anderson now had his turn with the witness. He was very direct and hammered away with questions. He took full advantage of the fact that Cercey was now on the stand so he questioned her at will. As I listened to him, I realized he is a remarkable prosecutor, one you definitely want on your side. I have since learned that before he retired, he was the top prosecutor in California to win death penalty convictions.

As Cercey was cross-examined by Anderson, a number of inconsistencies in her testimony were shown. She testified that she read very little of the transcript of her preliminary hearing testimony; instead, she admitted she tore it up. Earlier she said she had not discussed the case very much at all with defense counsel but now it was revealed she met with counsel five times. Also, she admitted she knew there was no moon that night; at the preliminary hearing she testified she didn't know whether there was a moon. And she didn't know whether the man who threatened to kill her looked like the blond-haired man she said she saw earlier by the dumpster.

After Cercey left the stand, Jim Anderson called three witnesses, all correctional officers who had problems with International when he was imprisoned. The first, James Ingram, was a Correctional Administrator for the Department of Corrections. I observed International never looked at Ingram while he was questioned.

On April 9, 1977, Ingram was employed at San Quentin as a Program Administrator and supervised the 2:00 o'clock meal in a section of the dining room reserved for Maximum B inmates (inmates assigned to a Special Housing Unit because of their behavior). Ingram said International came through the food line and asked for additional Jello. When told he already had his portion, International threw his food tray at Ingram. Ingram did not require medical treatment but International was removed from the service area and received a write-up on his record.

Warren F. Cawley, the next witness called by Anderson, was a correctional officer at the Deuel Vocational Institution. On February 13, 1976, while Cawley was on duty in the visiting room there, he warned International three times to stop sexually fondling his female visitor, a violation of the institution rules. Later, International approached Cawley and asked why he was "fucking with him." Cawley replied that he was only enforcing the rules. International said, "I'm going to kill you within the week," if he didn't leave him alone. Because his tone of voice and physical stance appeared serious, Cawley wrote him up, for which International received ten days in isolation.

Anderson's last witness was Raymond Kesner, a 20-year correctional officer. On March 15, 1977, he supervised the midday meal at San Quentin when International was denied a meal because he was late for lunch, having had an attorney visit. International became violent and insisted he was going to eat. He grabbed a tray, and helped himself to some pie. A tugging match developed and International hit Kesner in the jaw. An officer with a gun fired a shot and International froze. For this incident, he spent 10 days in isolation and lost 30 days of good time.

Chaffee did not counter with many questions for the three officers. It struck me it would be hard to defend International's vile behavior in these particular incidents. Also it appeared that when something did not go his way, International resorted to violence.

Judge Byers then discussed the court timetable. He told the jury to be back tomorrow, Thursday, June12th, and asked if any of them had a commitment for Friday. One had a family graduation so he announced that court would be held tomorrow but Friday and the weekend would be free. When I heard this, I was glad my reservation was for a week so I would be able to attend the entire second trial.

That evening, Jean and I headed over to the San Francisco airport to meet Gerry who was on a late flight. He was able to take some time off as a school psychologist at the Howard County (Maryland) Public Schools to join me at the trial. Gerry had been out at the Preliminary Hearing with me last October and had met Jean then. It was late so we headed back to Jean's home with the last boarder for the Stirpe Hotel. On the way, we reviewed what had taken place so far in this trial.

As Mary's oldest brother, Gerry had written a moving letter to Judge Byers at the start of the first trial.

> I am writing on behalf of my sister, Mary Gioia, one of the victims in the murder trial over which you are presiding. I am Mary's oldest brother by seven years. I am writing to tell you a bit about the person Mary was and to convey to you and the court the impact that Mary's death has had on myself and our family....
>
> During Mary's 22 years of life, she was a kind, caring and trusting person who was always quite willing to give of herself to others.... She was a happy person who tried as best she knew how to shed that happiness on others. Part of her special

nature I believe was an idealism about people and the world.... Over the years as Mary was growing up I would look toward her for her sweetness and innocence. This was symbolized so well in the cute little giggle and accompanying smile that she often gave. Her way was always a refreshing reminder to me of a very important aspect of life to preserve. This is one of the reasons why for Mary to die in such a violent, tragic way is a particularly terrible, terrible insult to what she believed in and how she lived her life.

As one of the oldest in our family of eight children, I could see how Mary symbolized the essence of hard work and determination along with kindness and compassion. Although Mary's strengths were not in "book-knowledge," as with many of her siblings, she still sought to develop her own talents to the fullest. Mary used her interest, talent, and creativity in baking to construct magnificent gingerbread houses and intricate chocolate figures for the family at Christmastime. I have fond memories of Mary's special nature in the way she cheerfully laughed off my mistake of eating part of her gingerbread creation one Christmas, only to have quickly reproduced it with such ease and willingness. She would send "care" packages to me at various times while in college, knowing how thrilled I was at receiving them.

Mary was also a creative artist, sketching pictures in her free time. A sketchbook of Mary's shows an assortment of sketches of flowers, which I believe symbolized to her the beauty and delicacy in life. In fact, Mary drew the beautiful rose that was on the cover of our wedding booklet last May. As you can see, Mary was a special young lady with many talents that she was always willing to share with others.

22

THE PENALTY PHASE CONTINUES

Thursday, June 12th - Gerry, now my VW Bug driver, and I went down to the courthouse in the morning after breakfast. I introduced him to David and Dorothy, already there. We prepared ourselves for another day of testimony.

Jim Anderson began by entering International's twelve previous convictions into the court record. Although all of these crimes had been referenced in Defense Counsel Susan Walsh's opening statement, each time they were recited emphasized International's proclivity for violence. He sought complete control over his victims in those crimes and used a gun to force them to perform sexual acts on him and his partner.

Jim Chaffee called his first witness, Marshall Perkins, employed at San Quentin Prison before his retirement. Chaffee asked Perkins' interpretation of the incidents recited by Anderson's witnesses, the three correctional officers, seeking to have them viewed as minor infractions. Perkins recalled that International worked in the prison bakery and said he could only work there if considered a reliable prisoner. Perkins did not know of any gang involvement by International while in prison and, in 1984, after International was out of prison, Perkins hired him to work part-time in his tree maintenance business.

Next, Chaffee called upon Hattie Henderson, International's mother, who now lived in Texas, about 75 miles west of Houston. She said she had five children, four still living. Her son, Ralph Thomas, Jr., was born on June 14, 1954. She separated from her husband when International was about 4 years old.

Mrs. Henderson attended several days of the first trial. When the defense saw that Mary's family, as well as Greg's, were represented in the courtroom, he put out the call for International's family. Mrs. Henderson and her daughter began to attend the court sessions. I found it difficult to look over at them, especially his mother. I knew she loved her son as I loved my daughter. All during the trials, I never spoke to her—I couldn't. My emotions were very raw and I wasn't sure how I would react. Perhaps if we met now, it might be different. We are two mothers who still suffer.

Chaffee continued to question Mrs. Henderson about International's childhood and his school years. She said he attended school through the 6th grade and adjusted "real good." When he was 12 or 13 years old, though, he ran away from home and after she reported it to the police, he was found in Tucson, Arizona.

Chaffee showed her a photograph of Ralph as a Boy Scout, about 11 years old. She explained that he received several scouting awards for being heroic; one for saving a little boy from drowning. As Chaffee questioned her, she revealed she was a strict disciplinarian and raised her children with the Bible.

After International ran away, she put him in a "boys' camp" for a few months. But then he ran away from the camp— he was 13 years old. When he telephoned her, he said he wanted to be on his own. She finally accepted this but told him to call when he needed something. She heard from him in the fall of 1967. He was then in California.

Jim Anderson approached International's mother on the stand and asked, "Mrs. Henderson, you obviously love your son, don't you?" She replied, "Yes."

Anderson: "Thank you very much, no further questions."

Chaffee's next witness was Emma Allen, International's sister. As the oldest of five children, she helped her mother take care of the others when her mother worked. She said she graduated from high school. As a boy, International was "no problem at all." She said he ran away because he didn't like living in Houston and missed doing things with his father when his parents separated.

Jim Anderson, when he questioned Allen, concentrated on the Boy Scout award International had received when he saved a young boy from drowning. Anderson noted that it must have been quite a topic of conversation at their house, as well as the house of the boy he saved. When he asked Allen the last name of the boy International had saved, she did not know it, nor did she know his first name.

With Chaffee's witnesses finished, Judge Byers announced that the testimony phase of the trial was over. He adjourned court until 11am on Monday and again warned the jurors to stay away from newspapers, televisions, or anyone who might report on the trial. The alternates were directed not to discuss anything with the twelve jurors.

Since it was only late morning, Gerry said, "Mom, how about we take a drive down the coast along Highway 1. I'll show you where Marge and I stayed on our honeymoon in Big Sur. It's a beautiful place, and I think we could both use a little R & R."

We said brief goodbyes to David and Dorothy and we headed out for our southern excursion. We crossed the San Mateo Bridge, drove over to Half Moon Bay and on to Highway 1, which would take us down the coast. As we drove, it was hard not to marvel at the spectacular beauty of California's coastline. We drove by Santa Cruz, where Jean and I had explored a few weeks earlier, and then continued past Monterey, Pebble Beach, and finally arrived at Carmel-By-The-Sea.

We stopped for lunch at a restaurant in Carmel. One caught our eye, as it resembled an old hunting lodge, with dark brown painted logs on its exterior. The sign read, "Hog's Breath Inn." A crowd waited at the front door, as well as inside. We learned its owner was actor Clint Eastwood, then Mayor of Carmel. We knew it would be a wait to be seated, but it would make for great conversation later on to tell everyone we ate in Clint Eastwood's restaurant. Before we entered, I made a pact with Gerry. "There's no way I can spend my good 'Democratically-earned' money in a place owned by this Republican, so, if we go in, this tab is on you." I may have been only half-serious, but Gerry, being quite hungry, quickly accepted.

Our meal together was an opportune time to talk about our feelings on this phase of the trial and to discuss other things occurring in our lives. Gerry was recently accepted into a post-doctoral program at Children's Hospital in Boston. He was excited about this latest step in his career and would start there next month. It felt good to have some positive events that we could look forward to, as we had expended so much of our communal energy on getting through this last year.

Gerry, in his impact letter to Judge Byers, explained how Mary's death had affected him.

> I know that I have been deeply affected in both my personal and professional life by the loss of my sister Mary. Her death has been such a senseless loss that I continue to struggle with and try to place it into a healthy perspective. I am a child psychologist by training and believe that an important part of my own work is to maintain a sense of caring and optimism with regard to mankind seeking a better life. Mary's murder has made me question some of the most basic aspects of human existence. I'm not quite as sure about people's true motivations anymore. I also have less trust in human nature. I feel a deep sense of anger that a refreshing and innocent part of our world can be, and has been, so violently erased by the selfish, deranged and disturbed behavior of another.

> Our whole family is still grasping for a way to understand all of this and to live our lives happily without our sister. We are all strong people and have a tight family unit which has helped, but it is still very, very difficult to fully accept this tragic loss. I know these feelings will stay with us our entire lives and that we will miss Mary terribly.

> I hope that I have provided for you some idea of who my sister, Mary Gioia, was during her lifetime and the significance of her loss on myself and my family. Although nothing will be able to bring back our loving, caring sister, and the pain and loss will always be with us, maybe our world, and Mary's soul, will be consoled by knowing that justice will be served. I hope that the person responsible for this horrid act can be prevented from ever

committing such a crime again so that others do not
have to suffer as well.

After lunch, we headed back onto Highway 1, and followed it a little farther down to Big Sur. Just then, Gerry pulled the car over to the side of the road. "Mom, take a look at this. It's got to be one of the most spectacular views of the Pacific."

"Okay, Ger, you're right, but my head is dizzy just thinking about looking down. I'll peek out the window."

Parked there, upon that cliff, the ocean far below us, my chronic fear of heights was in full array. I froze to my seat, and there was no way that I would emerge from that car. I took a quick look, while my body leaned towards the safe middle of the VW.

A few minutes later, we arrived at the Big Sur Inn, where Gerry and Margie had stayed on their honeymoon, incredibly just one year before. The Inn appeared quite rustic; its rooms looked neat and comfortable. Gerry showed me the wonderful restaurant at the Inn that overlooked the ocean, where he and Margie had several great meals. As we moved around, a congenial young woman greeted us and inquired if we needed a room. She looked at us strangely as she saw a young man accompanied by a much more mature woman. Gerry quickly said, "Oh, I'm just showing my Mom where I spent my honeymoon last year." Even this made the young woman's eyes open wide. Not being able to resist, I piped up and said, "Yes, I always demand to see where my sons have gone on their honeymoon." The young woman smiled, finally realizing perhaps we were pulling her leg.

After our short tour of the Big Sur Inn, we headed back to Oakland. It had been a good break. I think I understand better now what Mary meant when she wrote, "If I listen for it, I hear the waves crashing in."

That night, Jean, Gerry and I ate in a delightful restaurant in Alameda that overlooked San Francisco Bay. It had a beautiful and peaceful view of the Bay. Somehow it seemed we're never too far away from this body of water that played such a major role in our lives.

Gerry left the next day, headed back to Maryland. Although the trial was not over, he needed to get ready for his move to Boston. It was good to have him out here with me, even if it was for a short time.

Jean and I spent the next few days relaxing, as much as was possible, before Monday when closing arguments were scheduled. On Saturday, we toured the Oakland Museum. Located near the courthouse, it offered an extraordinary look into the art, history, ecology and the people of California. The exhibits that detailed the history of the founding of the state were especially interesting and informative for an Easterner like me. In 2002, when I would return to Oakland to attend an evidentiary hearing on our case, I would spend a complete day wandering through the museum viewing an exhibit of Ansel Adams' photography and artwork celebrating Oakland's 150th anniversary.

On Saturday night, we went over to Berkeley for dinner and to see more of that unconventional city. A very strange happening occurred as we drove along the highway. I couldn't believe my eyes. Right there, next to us on the road, was a van painted in several bright colors, complete with Grateful Dead and peace symbols all over it. As we passed it, I saw who was driving. I gasped, "Jean, it's Vincent Johnson, from Rainbow Village, from the trial! He was the fellow who said Vivian Cercey admitted to him that she never saw anything that night." As we drove past him, it was like seeing an old friend but not being able to quite reach out and talk to him. We continued on our way, but I felt strongly that somehow we were supposed to have had this vision that night.

The next day, we went shopping in San Francisco. I needed to buy several gifts and mementos before I left California. It may seem strange that I would want to have mementos from this place that gave me so much pain. But it was the last place Mary had been, and she quickly recognized the beauty and charm of the area. Jean also persuaded me to purchase a dress - one that I would always remember as my California dress. In Macy's Department Store, after some searching, I finally chose a steel-blue two-piece dress, dotted with small pink roses. It remained my favorite outfit for many years. When I wore it, Jean was right, it reminded me of this place and our quest for justice for Mary.

23

THE END OF THE PENALTY PHASE

Monday, June 16th - I woke up and knew why I was tense. Today was the last day of the penalty trial—the pivotal moment we've awaited. I met David and Dorothy outside the courtroom. Jim Anderson immediately came over to us. An attractive, dark-haired, well-groomed woman, with a teen-age girl at her side, stood next to him. Jim smiled as he introduced us to his wife and daughter. When Jim left us to take his place at the table, Mrs. Anderson spoke to me. She said Jim seemed so involved and immersed in this case that she had to come to hear his closing arguments. I felt better hearing this. I knew Jim would give it his best shot, but now that appeared a certainty.

At that moment, the Judge and jury filed into the courtroom. Before the session began, Judge Byers entered two dates into the record: August 17, 1983, when International was released from prison to parole, and November 17, 1984, when he was discharged from parole.

With the stage set, Jim Anderson rose to begin his closing argument. He reminded the jury that whatever he said, and whatever Chaffee said, during these closings was not evidence. He told them he and Chaffee are advocates and, of course, want the jury to do whatever they say, but, in the end, it's up to them to decide International's fate. He said the purpose of this short trial is for them to weigh the aggravating against the mitigating circumstances. He reminded them that the aggravating circumstances are International's twelve prior felonies, his assaults on

186

the guards while in prison, and, of course, the two murders. Mitigating ones are Vivian Cercey's testimony, the one guard who thought International was "just another ordinary inmate," and the testimony from International's family.

At this point, Jim smoothly moved into his summation by telling the jurors Cercey was called back for one reason - to correct the testimony she gave at the preliminary hearing. He reminded them that she admitted she met with the defense team five times but said she never discussed the case.

> *Okay, now, let's look at some of her prior testimony that was read to you from the preliminary hearing and let's prove to you how indeed her testimony was shaped by facts she had gotten from somebody we'll never know or do you want to guess who it might have been?*
>
> *In November she doesn't know if there's any moon light out there that night. Enkerud testifies at the trial there was no moon and Miss Cercey at this penalty phase knows there's no moon light out tonight. She's met with the defense team five times and yet she now knows that there was a moonless night and the city of Berkeley hills provided the illumination of Rainbow Village. That's just amazing. That's just amazing. But she didn't discuss her case with anybody.*
>
> *Any lingering doubt based on her coached, penalty phase testimony, should be cast upon the winds. His guilt is now etched in stone, just about like the Ten Commandments.*

(The above quotes are from the Concurring Opinion of J. Panelli and four other Judges of the California Supreme Court, filed on April 23, 1992, pp. 64, 65.)

Anderson continued, asking rhetorically how many lights from the Berkeley hills could be on at 4 o'clock in the morning if this is what illuminated the area since there was no moon. Anderson said, "That's a crock." as he argued the defense wanted the jury to think they made a mistake in convicting

International, that the "blond guy" really did it. He then cited the defense's other mitigating circumstances: the testimony by International's mother, who loved him deeply, and that of his sister, who, although from a "close" family, could not remember the name of the boy who her brother saved from drowning.

Anderson argued that the scales to measure the aggravating and mitigating circumstances in this case were grossly disproportional and reminded the jury that each one of them had said, when questioned before the trial, that they could vote for the death penalty if it came to that. Before he concluded his argument, he threw in another consideration. If International is not segregated on to death row, would the prison guards at San Quentin be safe? If, under life without parole, he harmed a guard, he would have nothing to lose. Anderson described it as "open season on the guards at San Quentin." His final statement was "Death row has got to be his final home."

As I heard Jim Anderson's final words, I shuddered. The inference to death row as International's final home was a stark but firm statement. I felt Anderson's arguments were logical and that, once again, he put his whole heart and soul into his remarks to achieve justice for our kids.

Jim Chaffee, the Public Defender, now rose to present his closing arguments to save International from death. He addressed the jury: "We're not talking about death versus freedom. We're talking about death versus life in prison without parole." He reminded them that Judge Byers told them they might have lingering doubt and that a greater degree of certainty, *without the slightest chance of being wrong*, was needed before they could impose the death penalty. And he reminded the jury that, in this case, there was no reliable witness who saw it, nor a reliable confession that someone actually did it.

Chaffee pointed out that International was about 20 years of age when convicted of those other crimes and the fact that he had a firearm didn't mean he used it. He didn't shoot anybody; he didn't hurt anybody. Hearing this, I thought, *didn't hurt anybody?* That his previous victims could not sit in the same room with him, told me that they still suffer from their encounters with him. They will be forever scarred by those vicious crimes.

Chaffee continued and said there were no serious injuries to the correctional guards that International had threatened or fought with. He questioned that this would be enough to now sentence him to death. And he reminded the jury that when International was incarcerated at San Quentin, he wasn't involved with gangs; he just minded his own business.

Chaffee, in a last attempt to save International, suggested to the jurors that "a year from now, two years, or ten, you might walk the floor at three in the morning and say, 'My God, what have I done?'"

A short recess took place and then Jim Anderson had one more appeal to the jury. In his earlier remarks, he told the jury that "your sympathies should go to all the victims of the defendant's depraved past and present...." Judge Byers overruled Chaffee's objection to this statement. Now Jim urged the jury to "have sympathy also for the families of Mary Gioia and Greg Kniffin, because their lives are never going to be the same." He concluded by saying he hoped that Mary and Greg did not suffer when the defendant shot them. Those words tugged at my heart. I tried hard not to burst into tears at that image. Once again, I held Mary's photo in my lap. I knew it was her spirit that helped me through all of this; she was my rock.

The jurors did not have an easy task. They spoke about their concerns: the consequences of their penalty determination and if they failed to reach a unanimous decision. They requested "a clarification of the appeal aspects of our decision, as in a death sentence. Can it be appealed and continued through the judicial system for years? Is a sentence of life without possibility of parole also subject to appeal and challenge, or is it essentially irrevocable?" As I listened to their questions, I realized this jury would be fair, no matter what their decision would be.

The Judge responded: "Anyone convicted of a crime, no matter what penalty is given, has appellate rights. However, it would be a violation of the jurors' duty to consider defendant's appellate rights in determining the appropriate sentence in this case. You are not to concern yourself." Both the prosecutor and the defense agreed.

Regarding their question: "What would be the action

taken by the court in the event that the jury is unable to reach a unanimous decision," they are told: "That again is not for the jury to consider or to concern itself with. You must make every effort to reach a unanimous decision if at all possible."

My witness for Mary was now over. As soon as the closing arguments concluded, I returned home. International had been convicted. No matter which sentence the jurors decided upon, he will be in prison for the rest of his life. However, my heart remained heavy. Mary would always be gone.

Friday, June 20th - We received the news. After five days of deliberation, the jury ruled out a possible life term in state prison, without possibility of parole. They decided Ralph International Thomas should die in San Quentin's gas chamber. I received the telephone call, while at work, from an excited Jim Anderson. He was happy with the jury's decision but he knew that it was also bittersweet for Mary and Greg's families. I thanked him for all his hard work during the trials and acknowledged that although he always maintained that tough outer demeanor of a prosecutor, I knew down deep he harbored immense compassion for the families of murdered victims.

After hearing this great news, I needed to do something – somehow I had to acknowledge this day. On my way home from work, I stopped at Yonder Farms, a combination nursery and gift shop, and a favorite place of Mary's. She often stopped there to purchase a card, a plant, or other small gift on her way back to Schenectady from Albany. I looked around its inventory of treasures and finally found what I wanted. It was a small stone plaque with a rose engraved on it. I then drove to the cemetery, knelt at her grave, the tears streaming down. I spoke to her, "Okay, Mare, rest in peace, the monster has been convicted and sentenced to death."

June 20th was also Joan's birthday. It had been one year since Mary made that delicious carrot cake for her. This decision was a birthday gift to her. She now knew that the man who murdered her little sister would finally be punished.

24

THE MONTHS AFTER THE TRIALS

With the two trials now over, International's sentencing was set for August 21st. Jean sent me articles on the jury's decision that appeared in the California newspapers. As I read them, I felt I was out there for the awaited decision.

> *Ralph International Thomas should die in San Quentin's gas chamber for killing a man and a woman last year on the Berkeley waterfront, an Alameda County jury decided yesterday in Oakland.*
>
> *Superior Court Judge Robert K. Byers will sentence Thomas, 32, on Aug. 21. By law, Byers must review the case, and Thomas gets an automatic appeal to the state Supreme Court.*
>
> *...No one saw the killings. The most influential evidence, said jury foreman Ronald Parker of Oakland, was that Thomas owned a .44-caliber magnum rifle and was seen with the victims at 2 a.m. Aug. 16, the day of the killings, after a party at the village.*
>
> *...Parker said jurors were influenced strongly by the "heinous" nature of the crime. Thomas did not have a magazine for the ammunition and would have had to reload between the killings. This was the "key" factor in both the conviction and penalty decisions, he said.*

Parker said jurors noted that Thomas was seen walking from the area of the murders at 6:30 a.m. Aug. 16. "The site really had been cleaned up," Parker observed.

Jurors in varying degrees also took into account Thomas' record of violence, Parker said.

...Parker, a 45-year-old accountant, said jurors disregarded what they considered the "contradictory" testimony of a woman who said she saw a blond man with Gioia and Kniffin shortly before hearing three "noises like firecrackers."

Spears, Larry. Jury urges death for killer of two. The Tribune, June 21, 1986.

Another newspaper described International's demeanor in court that day.

Thomas, bearded and wearing his shaggy hair in braids, sat impassively as the death verdict was read.

He quietly laughed and spoke softly to his defense team after the jury filed out of the heavily guarded courtroom.

...During the penalty phase, prosecutor James Anderson told the jury of Thomas' previous convictions stemming from the kidnapping and sexual abuse of two women hitchhikers in Alameda County and two in Monterey County.

In all cases, the victims were taken to the Santa Cruz Mountains and repeatedly raped at gunpoint, said the deputy district attorney.

Referring to Thomas' 12 prior convictions – including kidnapping, rape, sodomy and forced oral copulation – Anderson said that Thomas "had already committed some of the most heinous crimes the penal code has to offer" before the murders.

... " I think the death penalty is more than adequate because of his reprehensible background," Anderson said yesterday. "Maybe the four rape victims will read about this in the newspaper and think

that justice has now been served."

Assistant Public Defender Susan Walsh, who focused on Thomas' disadvantaged upbringing in Houston during the penalty phase, had no comment to yesterday's decision by the jury.

Martinez, Don. Jury wants Rainbow Village killer executed. The Examiner, June 21, 1986.

It was time to thank some people who contributed to the conviction of Mary and Greg's murderer. On June 30th, I wrote to Jim Anderson regarding his superb job:

Now that I am back home in New York, I want to let you know how grateful I and my whole family are to you for bringing to a successful conclusion the trial and conviction of Ralph International Thomas. The guilty verdict by the jury and its subsequent recommendation to the Judge of the death penalty are, in our opinion, as far as the criminal justice system could possibly go in bringing some semblance of justice for the brutal murders of Mary and Greg.

I also want to thank you for doing all you possibly could do—under the stricture of California laws—to allow David and myself to participate in the proceedings as the victims' families. I appreciate the compassion you showed us and know you respected our feeling of utter frustration when we wanted to have more input.

I am writing also to Dan Wolke and Fred Eihl to thank them for their excellent investigative work—and to Stephanie Lynch who worked with us since the very beginning of this nightmare and helped us cope emotionally and also provided us with useful information when we needed it.

I want to thank you especially for making Mary and Greg real persons to the jury during the trial and for displaying the pictures of these two beautiful kids on several occasions.

I was very moved when at the penalty trial you asked the jury to have sympathy for Mary and Greg and their families, especially when they were being asked over and over by the Defense to have sympathy for International. Mary's spirit was with me throughout the trial. I always felt she was with me—right there in the courtroom—helping me to get through it. I know she is saying thank you to you, Jim, because, hopefully, International will never ever be able to hurt anyone again.

I realize Judge Byers will be announcing the sentence on August 21st. I can't believe he could come to any other decision than that already suggested by the jury.

Again, from all of us, thank you.

P.S. Thought you'd enjoy the card!

The postscript referred to a "Thank You" card Gerry and I found when we were in Carmel. It showed a cowboy, resembling Clint Eastwood, saying, "Make My Day!" I sent it to Jim telling him he had made "The Gioia's Day" by accomplishing the marvelous conviction of International.

That July, Gerry and Margie moved to Boston as Gerry was to start his post-doctoral training in neuropsychology at Children's Hospital. He put out the call to the family for help with their move. Many of us responded, and it provided another opportunity for us to be together. Those first years after Mary's death were especially difficult for all of us. Just being together helped us to imagine that we were once again a complete family.

Joan, now eight months pregnant, her husband, Mike, and I drove over to Boston for the 4th of July weekend. Margie and Gerry rented a U-Haul truck and met us at their West Roxbury apartment. While the men moved the furniture into the apartment and set it up, Christine, Margie and I performed some lighter tasks, such as putting contact paper on a myriad of shelves for their dishes and food. Joan sported a brace on her arm so she was excused from that task.

When the apartment was in good shape, we shared a meal together. Mary was much in our thoughts, and we reminisced about her trip to Boston a few years before. I think all of us wished she had remained here; perhaps then she never would have gone to California.

A month later, a joyous event occurred. Joan's second child, Michael Vito (named after his father and two grandfathers) arrived on August 7th. It was a wonderful celebration of new life in our family.

Despite our delight with baby Michael, a date we all dreaded - August 16th – approached. It would be the first anniversary of Mary's death. It was as if a large black hole loomed on the horizon that none of us wanted to confront. A few days before, Gerry called with a suggestion.

"Mom, I know it's going to be a really hard time for all of us, so why don't we concentrate on some pleasant memories we have of Mary. Let's get together, sit around, and talk about her. I'm sure everyone has a memory, a story, that could be shared."

"Good idea. You're right; somehow, we have to be able to turn this terrible, sad day into something more positive, a celebration of her life. Maybe have some music, compliments of Patrick, Lawrence and Robert."

That is exactly what we did. On that Saturday afternoon, Mary's First Anniversary, we all gathered in the living room of the old family homestead. I can't remember who started it off but as we went around the room, everyone had a story, a tale about Mary they shared. Some were old favorites we'd heard over the years, such as the gingerbread house door Gerry mistakenly ate, Lawr's adventures teaching her to drive, her boxing Danny's ears when he made her mad. Danny brought a smile to all our faces and a few tears as he told how when he saw Mary sitting out on the front porch swing, dressed in her long skirt, bandana and Birkenstocks, he said, "Gee, Mare, we're going to a Yankee game, not a Dead concert!" Christine, the birthday sister, told us again that when Pat and Rob told her about Mary's death, she cried, "I'll never have another birthday!"

The stories went on and on and we felt that Mary somehow was right there with us. After this, we all headed over to Park View Cemetery and placed a bouquet of roses at her grave. When Rob and Patrick started to strum "Ripple" and "Forever Young," there were few dry eyes. Somehow we got through that day, but we knew our lives would never be the same. Our loss of

Mary would always play a big part.

A dear friend, Rita Boyd, joined us for this anniversary. Rita and I were friends since high school days in Queens, New York. We lost touch with each other, after our marriages, but resumed our friendship a few years before Mary's death. Rita learned about Mary's death from another good friend, Betty. When we connected, I learned Rita's 25-year-old son, Michael, had taken his own life in December of 1985, just four months after Mary's death. I knew Rita, too, suffered greatly by Michael's death. I invited her to join us that day when we celebrated Mary's life. It would also be a celebration of Michael's.

A few days after her visit, Rita wrote:

> *I want to put down a few of the thoughts and deep feelings that came to me this weekend— with you and your family. First how much I appreciated being with you all.*
>
> *– I felt part of your sorrow and the joy of living you and your family give out. One of the difficulties I suffered last spring was extreme loneliness—no one to share my thoughts and feelings about Michael with. It was a great longing and desperation so I am grateful to have time sharing feelings and memories and the pangs of loss of Michael and your Mary. You all know how it is.*
>
> *My children, Lizzie and Michael, would have loved her. They found the hard-edged, hi-tech plastics world of the eighties oppressive. Mary's "flower" child embrace of whole earth values and life style through her crafts and baking would have been a bond. Michael said he wanted to stay a kid, but what I really think is that he, perhaps like Mary, hated to see the LOVE power and anti-establishmentarianism and positive side of the Sixties "revolution" disappear.*

Rita and I remain close friends. Each year, she remembers Mary's anniversary and I, as well, remember her dear Michael's anniversary. Both of us know that a loss of a child is like no other.

25

INTERNATIONAL IS SENTENCED

We anxiously awaited the sentencing, scheduled for August 21st. Jim Anderson advised us that International's attorneys had prepared arguments to reduce the jury's finding of first degree murder to second degree murder. This delayed the sentencing and prolonged our distress.

On September 4th, the motion was denied. Jean sent me an article that reported on this development.

> Sentencing of Ralph International Thomas, found guilty of two murders and recommended for the death penalty, was delayed for three weeks yesterday to give his attorneys time to prepare arguments against sending him to the gas chamber.
>
> "He shot their heads off with a .44-caliber Magnum," said a sentencing report by Edward Hall, a deputy Alameda County probation officer. "He dumped both of them into the estuary."
>
> ...Hall's report said Thomas was seen arguing with the couple for unknown reasons.
>
> Asked by Berkeley police about his .44 rifle, he told them it had been stolen, then later asked a neighbor to hide his rifle case, cleaning kit and some ammunition. The weapon has never been found.
>
> ...If (Judge) Byers finds the jury's recommendation (of the death penalty) unwarranted, he can reduce the sentence to life without parole.

Hall's report did not recommend the lower sentence. (emphasis added)

The report said Thomas continues to maintain his innocence, contending he was convicted because of his prior record, which the jury did not learn of until after they voted to convict, and because he could not afford to pay an attorney.

Lane, Del. Rainbow Village killer's lawyers trying to save him from death. <u>The Tribune</u>, September 5, 1986.

At this time, I decided to write a second impact letter to Judge Byers. I originally sent one on May 1, before the trial began. I realized he probably did not read it until after both trials were concluded. Now I had more to tell him, more to say.

I write once again as you prepare to sentence Ralph Thomas. I had believed this was to take place last Thursday but know that another brief has been entered by the Public Defender which requires your review.

I wish I could be present in the courtroom for the sentencing, as I was for every minute of the two trials. But California is too far away. I am glad that I did attend the trials so that the full story surrounding these horrendous murders could somehow be grasped. I also felt it was the ONLY thing I could do for my daughter, Mary Regina—just to be there for her..

My family—all of Mary's sisters and brothers gathered together in my home on August 16th of this year to celebrate Mary's life and what she meant to all of us. We also wanted to confront the anniversary of her death—to be together to console each other. We have "gotten through" this year of pain, frustration and anger but it has taken its toll on all of us.

I am particularly angered by the flyer I understand is being circulated outside the Court House in Oakland indicating racial overtones to the trial and sentencing of Ralph Thomas.

I find this charge of racism totally absurd and I hope all who read it will also. The skin color of this defendant and the victims had nothing to do with the guilty verdict by the jury.

The only way I can deal with Mary's death in my own life is to continue to be active in victims' groups and to try to help others who may experience the crime of homicide. I have been involved for many years with RID (Remove Intoxicated Drivers), a grass-roots action-oriented organization to stop the crime of driving while intoxicated. I am now working with Parents Of Murdered Children, a self-help group for families of homicide victims, and Victims of Crime Advocacy League of New York State. One can never fully recover from—or even grasp intellectually the full reality of—the murder of one's child.

However, I refuse to allow Ralph Thomas to also murder all of the hopes and joys of the Gioia family. We will go on, missing Mary, but knowing that she would want us to do so.

When I learned of Ralph Thomas' prior heinous felonies and his nine-year incarceration which seems to have utterly failed in rehabilitating him, I become angry at the criminal justice system which allows someone like him out on the streets again to harm and kill other innocent people. The recommendation of the death penalty by the jury is, in my opinion, the only way to insure that he will never hurt anyone again.

Thank you for reading and considering this statement.

The flyer I referred to in the letter had been distributed at the courthouse by Harry Shorman and some others. In bold letters it read:

SUPERIOR COURT JUDGE K. BYERS will sentence Ralph on August 21, 1986

RALPH INTERNATIONAL THOMAS RAILROADED by RACISIM to the GAS CHAMBER.

Should Ralph, 32, die for the killings of Gregory Kniffin, 18, and Mary Regina Gioia, 22, just because they are white and he is black?! An eye witness, a white woman, testified that she saw and heard a white man with blond hair named "Bo" arguing with the white couple just before they were killed in "Rainbow Village," Berkeley, August 1985. All evidence against Ralph was circumstantial. No one saw the killings.

NO WEAPON WAS EVER FOUND!

Is this enough to send a man to his death? No!!!

FREE RALPH!

Paid for by the F.R.E.E. COMMITTEE (Free Ralph from Easy Execution) 7/86

On September 25, 1986, Alameda County Superior Court Judge Robert K. Byers sentenced Ralph International Thomas to death.

...Ralph International Thomas was sentenced to death for the first-degree murder of Gregory Kniffin and 15 years to life for the second-degree slaying of Mary Regina Gioia in August 1985.

Thomas, 32, did not react when Alameda County Superior Court Judge Robert K. Byers announced the sentence.

In imposing the death penalty, Byers said the killings were "brutal, cold-blooded and without reasons." He said Thomas had no "social redeeming quality in his whole life." Byers called Thomas "an extremely dangerous person" who should "never be released from custody," even if the death sentence is overturned by the state Supreme Court. Death sentences are automatically appealed to the Supreme Court.

If Thomas' sentence is overturned or commuted to life, he would still have to serve time for the second-degree conviction.

Noting his extensive criminal record, Byers said Thomas on four previous occasions sexually attacked women and "has destroyed or harmed the lives of 46 other persons."

...At yesterday's sentencing, defense attorney James H. Chaffee, of the Public Defender's office, made an impassioned plea for the judge to spare Thomas' life. Chaffee argued that the death penalty should not be imposed when there is a question of whether the accused actually committed the crime.

He said Thomas was convicted on "circumstantial evidence" rather than evidence from "creditable eyewitnesses or a creditable confession" from the accused. He said the prosecutor had neither an eyewitness, a confession, a motive nor was the murder weapon produced.

Anderson, however, urged the judge to "show no mercy for a 14-time loser."

Jones, Will. Man sentenced to die for two 1985 murders. Rainbow Village slayings called 'cold-blooded.' The Oakland Tribune, *Sept. 26, 1986, D-4.*

Jim Anderson sent that news article to me with his letter of October 8, 1986.

Dear Pat,

Just thought I'd send the local news media account of the vermin responsible for causing so much unhappiness. As you recall, I told you Byers would not upset the jury verdict. As you can see, he thinks as much of Ralph I. Thomas as we do.

Once again, I know your loss is devastating beyond description, and I know how difficult it must have been for you to sit through the whole heartbreaking mess. However, don't think for one second that I didn't appreciate your care and feelings. I'm convinced that your and David's daily attendance contributed to the magnificent verdict—I really mean that. The death penalty won't bring Mary or Gregory back—but it will sure ruin Ralph's life!

Take care of yourself—I'm only sorry that we had to meet each other under such heartbreaking circumstances.

Thanks for your support.

Jim Anderson

The Gioia family all experienced a sense of relief that this horrible chapter of our lives finally came to conclusion. The trials were over, International was convicted and sentenced. But with a death penalty conviction, the case is never completely over. There would be endless appeals.

26

THE NEXT FEW YEARS

The trials, the sentencing, the trips to California were now over. Life has a way of going on, even when we're not ready for it. We were all at different crossroads in our lives but as a family we were determined that Mary's spirit would remain alive.

One day Joan called me at work. Her voice was hesitant so I knew she had something important to say.

"Mom, I won't be able to go to the POMC meeting tonight. In fact, I probably won't be able to go much anymore. With little Michael, and Amanda, and my work schedule, I just can't do it. I'll miss seeing everyone. I always felt more at peace when I came home from a meeting. But you can let me know what's going on."

"I understand, honey, your responsibility right now is to your family. I think we both know Mary wouldn't have it any other way."

Now attending the meetings alone, I immediately formed a deep bond with Robin Stambler, Chapter Leader and founder of the group, and with Bunni Vaughn, her sister and co-leader. Robin's daughter, Stephanie, was murdered in 1980; Robin never received justice in her case.

My fledgling victim advocacy had its start when Dr. Howard Velzy, a Methodist minister and co-founder of the Chapter, approached me after one of the meetings.

"Pat, we could really use you to work with VOCAL (Victims of Crime Advocacy League). It's a network of victims' organizations in New York State. Working for a State Senator could be helpful to us to monitor legislation. Last year, we succeeded in having the Fair Treatment Standards Act for Crime Victims finally passed but there's a lot more to be done." Howard was Chairman of VOCAL. His daughter, Linda, was murdered in 1977. Her murderer was sentenced to 25 years to life and has been denied parole each time he has become eligible.

Could I say no when asked to help crime victims? So I became active with VOCAL and slowly began to meet many others working for victims' rights. It seemed a positive way to release some of that anger I still harbored for Mary's brutal murder.

I became more aware of stories of local murders in the newspapers. Nothing opens up your eyes to crime faster than having someone you love murdered or otherwise violated by a crime. One day I read about a family member of a local murder victim who attended an out-of-state support group and found it helpful. I saw this as an informative opportunity and wrote a Letter to the Editor of the <u>Schenectady Gazette</u>:

> *"Much support can be derived by just talking to others who have experienced the same tragedy and have somehow 'come through' it. Sharing mutual experiences with the criminal justice system can also be helpful, especially for the newly victimized who are now thrust into what can be a totally new and confusing situation – dealing with district attorneys, the courts, trials, etc."*

I closed with contact information for our local POMC Chapter.

Telling Mary's story in a familiar setting at our POMC meetings with folks who well understood was a frequent activity, but up to this time, I had never written about it. When I attempted to do so, it was very painful. The words on the paper shouted back at me with terrible finality.

One day after work I stopped at the Albany Public Library. A small notice posted on a bulletin board caught my eye. A non-fiction prose workshop, "Risky Writing," was to begin the next week. Should I attend? I had no idea what risky writing was. I soon found out that there's a whole world of people out there who have had incidents in their lives that unless confronted could tear them apart. Now, with the encouragement of the leader and others, I finally wrote Mary's story. "Finished Business?" was reprinted in the Winter 1988 VOCAL newsletter, *Victims' Voice*. I too had found my voice.

On Sunday, May 1, 1988, the steps of the New York State Capitol were the unlikely setting for "A Day For Victims," as the first Crime Victims' Rights activity was held in the Capital District. A light representing the Eternal Flame was displayed and roses dotted the Capitol steps. POMC and VOCAL, along with RID, Albany County Rape Crisis Center, the Michele E. Martin Memorial Trust, and the Albany County STOP-DWI held planning meetings for a few months, most in my Senator's office after hours. We decided it was time the Capital District increase public awareness about the needs of crime victims. It was my honor to give the welcoming remarks and introduce the many speakers we had lined up. This was the humble start of the commemoration of National Crime Victims' Rights Week in the Capital District, continuing each year.

In October of 1991, the New York State Assembly Standing Committee on Governmental Operations held a hearing on the New York State Crime Victims' Board (CVB) and the delivery of victims' services in New York State. Howard gave a statement as Chairman of the Board of Directors of VOCAL and asked if I would also speak. I was fortunate that Senator Leichter not only permitted, but encouraged, me to participate in my crime victim advocacy when I worked for him. He recognized how important it was for me. I spoke not as an employee of the State Senate that day but as a member of POMC and the mother of a crime victim.

At the time (1991), there was a large backlog of victims' compensation claims in CVB. In my statement, I said:

> *Hardly a POMC meeting goes by without someone reporting their tale of woe. ...there seems to be lack of knowledge about the CVB and confusion over who can be assisted by it.*
>
> *Some of the common questions asked by victims are: Should I go through the hassle of filling out this complicated application? Must I be practically indigent to have burial expenses paid? Will medical*

expenses be reimbursed? Do I, or anyone else in my family, qualify for counseling? Where should I go to get the proper counseling that I may need? How do I find out what is happening in my criminal court case?

At that point, I outlined what had happened to Mary at Berkeley and told of the excellent victim advocacy I received from the State of California. I concluded with:

The theme of this year's National Victims' Rights Week was "A New Balance."

This reflects the ongoing efforts of many in the victims' movement to equalize the rights of the innocent victim of crime with the rights of the person convicted of the crime. I think we have a way to go in New York State to achieve that balance.

Today, CVB has become a major player in the assistance given to New York State crime victims. It funds programs for crime victim advocates in most district attorneys' offices statewide, as well as other programs dealing with domestic violence, rape, child abuse, etc. Most of the questions I raised in my statement at that hearing have been answered in a positive way.

While I was becoming active as a crime victims' advocate, the other family members continued with their daily lives, and struggled with the loss of their sister. I telephoned Chris one night in early summer of 1987, to see how she was doing.

"Mom, work and things are generally okay, but I miss Mary so much. What am I going to do without my little birthday sister?"

"I know, we all miss her. At least here I've got the support of my POMC group. You and the boys there in Boston don't have that. Listen, Robin and Bunni are encouraging me to go to the conference POMC is holding in August. Why don't you come with me?"

That August Chris and I attended the First National Conference of POMC in Cincinnati, Ohio. It was the first time both of us met so many others affected by homicide. Most had strong and angry feelings when they spoke about the person who murdered their loved one. But at one workshop, it almost came to blows when a mother, who chose to meet with and forgive her family member's murderer, tried to push her point of view on the rest of us. We all handle tragedy in our own way; no one can force their philosophy on others.

Upon returning to Boston, Chris attended her first POMC meeting. She had met some of the folks at the conference. Later she related her feelings about the experience, "Mom, there were so many people gathered around the table that night. Each told their own story of what happened to their loved one. I felt really overwhelmed. I went that once but haven't gone back." But she collected donations and walked in the first 7.5 mile Annual Walk to Protect Our Children, through the streets of Boston, on October 24, 1987, sponsored by the Adam Walsh Child Resource Center.

Although she never attended any more POMC meetings in Boston, when Chris moved back to Schenectady, she often accompanied me to mine. When a co-worker's sister was murdered, Chris quickly introduced her to POMC where she received support.

POMC had become my savior. It was there I could pour out my feelings to others who understood. But at the end of 1988, Robin and Bunni announced they were resigning their leadership of the Chapter.

"What's going to happen with our POMC group?" I asked.

The answer, "We could have an occasional meeting, or if after a murder a new family calls for help, a meeting could be held" didn't sound to me like a workable solution. I felt strongly that the continuity of meetings was paramount to help families of homicide victims. So I jumped up and said I would take over the Chapter for a while. That "while" has lasted until the present time. Many other good people along the way have helped to keep our Chapter going strong—but that is another story.

During those first years after Mary's death, despite the sadness we still experienced, our family celebrated several joyous events. I traveled over to Boston more frequently to be with that Gioia contingent. During the weekend of Gerry's birthday, in February of 1987, Rob and Brenda announced their wedding plans for the next summer.

On July 11, 1987, Robert and Brenda were married in Herkimer. It was a full weekend celebration. My brother, Marty and his son, Marty Jan, came up from Florida. Lawr and Mary Ann were the only family members missing as they awaited the imminent birth of their first child, Laura Elizabeth, who arrived on July 18.

The wedding was held in Brenda's family church in Herkimer. Several of Rob's friends played music at the ceremony. As I sat in the pew, quite proud and admiring the handsome couple at the altar, I heard some familiar strands of music strummed on the guitars. It was "Ripple," the Grateful Dead tune Rob performed at Mary's Memorial. As this haunting melody began, Rob turned around from his place at the altar, looked at me and smiled. The rest of the family glanced at one another, dabbing their eyes as the tears began to flow. We all knew at that moment, our Mary was right there with us.

Later that year, I made the painful decision to sell our big house on Cornelius Avenue. The aging house was now too much for me to handle alone. I knew it would be a difficult time for all of us.

Clearing out the house after 30 years of living there was a major effort. Joan's husband, Mike, and his brothers, moved our second-hand upright piano—the one I had antiqued a turquoise-blue—through the front door onto a waiting pickup truck. Many fond memories of Joan, Lawr and Mary as they sat practicing at that old piano went out the door with it that day.

It was time now to finally tackle clearing out Mary's belongings still remaining in the third floor bedroom. Chris chose a few pieces of jewelry and taking a full-length flowered dress from the closet, she said, "I remember Mary wearing this. It was just perfect for her. When I wear it, there'll be a little piece of her always with me."

Patrick grabbed her Grateful Dead concert stubs that were tucked into a box in a drawer, saying "I'll take these. We went to a few of these concerts together, right Rob? They will be a real reminder of our good times we had together." In later years, he placed them in a frame, displaying them with other Grateful Dead paraphernalia on his den wall.

After everyone chose what they wanted, there were a few things left which I kept. In a small metal candy box, originally from Worcestershire, England, she had stored some special treasures: the prescription for the heel lift she needed to correct her shorter leg; the mold of her teeth used for her braces; and a silver and red tassel, with a gold 81, the year she graduated from Niskayuna High School. Squirreled away also in there were her Learner's Permit, her seating card from Joan's wedding and a matchbook from Chris', and her Schenectady County Library card.

I then spotted her brown Tyrolean boots still in the closet. They brought back many memories of Mary, the young fun-loving girl, who loved to dress casual. I decided to keep them. Because they were quite sturdy, I often wore them while mowing my lawn. But in 1996, they were dispatched to Washington, DC for the Silent March, a lobby day held at the Capitol for effective gun laws. There, Mary's boots stood next to thousands of shoes, sneakers and boots of other gun violence victims. Each year, they return to Albany for the New Yorkers Against Gun Violence lobby day at the State Legislature. So Mary continues to speak out for peace and harmony in the world.

I also tucked away a silver ring bearing her initial "M." I often wear it when I attend an event honoring victims, or when I just want to feel closer to her.

As I turned to leave the room, I saw, carved into the windowsill, in small letters, the name, MARY. She left her mark on the house as well as our hearts.

The family gathered at 4 Cornelius that fall for one of our last times together at the house. It was Saturday, September 19th, 1987, and the University of Rochester football team, of which Dan was a co-captain, was to play Union College that afternoon in Schenectady. That year, Union had an exceptionally strong team and was favored to win. Leaving the house, we headed down to Union College and on the way into the field, several Union college students at the gate, greeted us saying, "Sorry, folks, Rochester doesn't stand a chance against us today."

Smiling, I quickly responded, "Oh, no? Just watch out for Number 22. That's my son, Dan Gioia, and he's determined to win today. After all, this is his hometown too."

And win, they did; the score was U of R 24, Union 20, with Dan, rushing for 145 yards. He could not be stopped! All of the family crowded into the stands, including three grandchildren. Robert videotaped most of the game, interspersing with amusing comments about our hero. That tape quickly became a family heirloom. I've always wondered if some of that winning spirit didn't spring from his sister.

After the game, that evening, Dan's whole football team (or so it seemed), his friends, his brothers' friends, and all the family, enjoyed the biggest Gioia lasagna feast ever at our house. Everyone made a tray of it. Gerry and Margie carried theirs on the plane from Maryland, its aroma teasing the other passengers! We were determined to enjoy our last hours together in the house. Patrick and Robert with the borrowed video camera captured "This Old House," going from room to room, starting at the basement and up to the third floor and attic. They described each room, giving classic scenarios of what it was like growing up there.

The next day, Sunday, we gathered together again as Lawr and Mary Ann's little Laura was baptized by our good friend, Bert Fay.

Christine's son, Sean, and Gerry's daughter, Theresa Rose, named after her Aunt Mary, were both born in September 1988, in Boston. A dual baptism was held during Thanksgiving weekend so all the family could attend and Bert Fay again presided. Margie provided everyone with Rod Stewart's newer version of "Forever Young," while Rob, Patrick and Lawr accompanied on guitar.

After the church service, a festive party celebrating the birth of the two new Gioia's took place in my new townhouse in the Town of Halfmoon. Kathleen, my goddaughter, and her two girls made the trip up from Florida to be with us.

Aunt Mary now had two more members of her family who would never know her. Over the years, as we celebrated many more happy family events, we always knew one member was missing. Yes, life does go on.

27

THE GRATEFUL DEAD CONCERT

MESSAGE TO DEADHEADS:
June, 1988
"When life looks like easy street
There is danger at your door"
…The Grateful Dead has an ugly, danger-
ous problem at its door, a situation bad enough to
put our future as a touring band in doubt. Part of
our audience—a small part, but that's all it takes—
is making us unwelcome at show site after show
site because of insensitive behavior, including fla-
grant consumption of illegal substances (including
alcohol), littering, and general disturbances of the
environment. More security or more rules aren't the
answer —you guys know what righteous behavior
is about. Because you created your scene, it is up to
you to preserve it.

This letter of warning to Dead Heads was distributed at
the Grateful Dead concert at Saratoga Performing Arts Center
(SPAC) on June 28, 1988. Joan and I were at that concert.

It reads as an ultimatum written by the head of a family.
Most families consist of those who make the rules, those who live
by the rules, and others who disobey the rules. As I entered SPAC
that day, I felt as if I was attending a big family reunion.

The moment I learned about the concert, I called Joan
and said "Flo Carson is trying to organize a group to attend the

SPAC Grateful Dead concert in memory of Mary. Dear Flo's suffering from a malignant cancer so she can't go. But how about if you and I go? Dan said he and some friends will be there too."

Joan, a bit surprised by her mother's sudden interest in attending a Dead concert, replied, "Mom, it sounds like a great idea, but do you know how hard it is to get tickets?"

"I do now that you're telling me. I'll try to work on it."

My mind moved into high gear. I recalled I knew the woman who worked at the Concourse ticket booth at the Empire State Plaza near my office. I telephoned her, explaining the reason I wanted to attend the concert. In a pleading tone, I asked, "Is there any way I could get tickets without standing on those crazy lines waiting for concert seats?"

She responded in a gracious manner, saying, "Okay, what I'll do is set aside two tickets for you. Stop by the window tomorrow around noon and they'll be ready. But, please don't tell a soul about this arrangement."

I thanked her and told her that this meant a great deal to my family and me.

The next day I found my way through the Concourse to pick up the promised tickets. Crowds of Dead Heads lined the walls that led to the ticket window. Some stood, some sat, all waiting patiently. Many of the young women reminded me of Mary, dressed in tie-dye blouses, long flowing skirts, bandanas covering their long hair, and, of course, Birkenstock sandals. A pang of guilt struck me but quickly disappeared as I told myself this was a mission I was on. When I reached the ticket window, my friend discreetly pushed the envelope to me containing two balcony tickets.

Still not satisfied, I thought if Mary couldn't be there, maybe, just maybe, the Grateful Dead would dedicate a song to her and Greg at the concert. Nobody, not even my Dead Head kids knew how I could get in touch with them. I telephoned a local rock station and they suggested I contact the Operations Manager at SPAC. Perhaps a message could be passed on to them that way.

When I reached the manager, I told him what I wanted to do. He listened attentively, and I believe sympathetically. He suggested I write a letter to the Grateful Dead and send it to his attention at SPAC. He assured me that he would forward the letter to the group, wherever they were at the time. But he said he could not promise that they would read my letter or that they would dedicate a song. Since this was the best I could do, it was certainly worth a try.

In my letter I said Mary had been one of their devoted fans and attended their 1985 SPAC concert. I asked if they would dedicate a song to Mary at their June 28th concert. I wrote:

> Mary was murdered in Berkeley, California, on August 16, 1985. A young man, Greg Kniffin (also a Deadhead), was murdered with her...She had been staying for a few days at Rainbow Village at the Berkeley Marina where Deadheads would stop for a few days...In her last letter, she told us she had seen your group at Ventura and was excited about seeing you at Lake Tahoe on August 24. But she never made the Tahoe concert because she and Greg were murdered by an evil, evil person, who was convicted and sentenced to death by the Oakland court. Mary had framed one of your songsheets, "Ripple." It hung in her room. At her Memorial service, her brother, Rob (also a Deadhead) played guitar and sang this song.
>
> I enclose a Memorial card. Mary drew this rose (I know it is one of your symbols) for her brother's wedding booklet. She also wrote the words (which I later discovered were from "China Doll") on the outside envelope of her last letter to us.
>
> I truly believe both Mary's and Greg's spirits will be dancing in the aisles to your music at this concert.

I told them I had never attended one of their concerts but that Mary's sister, Joan, and I would be at this one. Her brother, Dan, and many of their friends would be there too.

I mailed the letter and hoped for the best, knowing I was doing something that could be very painful. I could do no more.

The day of the concert, I left work early. Even Senator Leichter wished me luck as I left the office. As I drove home, appeals came over the radio for only ticket holders to come to

SPAC. Traffic was already backed up for miles. My heart pounded as I thought that maybe we wouldn't be able to get in to the concert.

I met Joan, and she drove up to SPAC. The radio was right. Everywhere you looked cars headed north - a mass evacuation to Saratoga. We heard the parking lot was already filled. Cars parked all along Route 50. We spotted a very small space between two cars. To our delight, two young men from New Hampshire moved their car a few feet and made room for ours, thus sparing us a two-mile trek to the concert.

We walked through the parking lot and arrived at the ticket booths. Suddenly I felt a gnawing, empty feeling in my gut. Joan and I looked at each other—no need to speak. We both knew. But, at that moment, a surge of strength and a feeling of inner peace came upon me. Yes, Mary's spirit was there; she was with us. And so we entered into the spirit of the concert, joining that family of Dead Heads.

I saw several of my sons' friends spread on blankets on the lawn, which was literally covered with people. I never saw so many at SPAC before. They saw us and immediately asked, "Are they going to play a song for Mary?" They too anxiously awaited the band's decision.

"We'll just have to see," I said, trying to remain positive. I knew it was now out of my hands.

Joan and I made our way to our seats in the balcony in the next to last row. We received some smiles, perhaps because I surely raised the mean age for someone attending a Grateful Dead concert!

During the show, I saw fairly well but sometimes had to stretch to look above or around some people who stood for most of the concert. We sat near several young men.

The one next to me smiled and said, "And which is this for you?"

I smiled back and responded, "And which is this for you?"

He quickly answered, "My 244th."

"Well, you have me beat by 243!"

At that, we were off on good footing and he helped me interpret what was going on during parts of the show. He lived on Long Island, was a psychologist, and said he recently went to a Dead Concert in New Jersey with his mother. "All mothers should go to a Dead Concert at least once." I agreed.

I was almost unaware that the group had taken the stage when the excitement and screaming began. My new friend loaned me his binoculars to see their faces. Jerry Garcia wore a black pantsuit, his gray hair flying about a prematurely aging face. He appeared heavier than I imagined he would be. He looked barefoot but my neighbor assured me he usually wore low-strung sandals. The other lead singer, Bob Weir, was a contrast to Jerry, having an athletic torso and wearing shorts. The audience went wild as he sang, moving back and forth across the stage, his hair shaking wildly. The white-haired drummer played a number of long and loud solos, most of which did nothing for my ears.

After the first few numbers were played, with no introduction or interaction with the audience, I started to doubt that a song would be dedicated to Mary and Greg that night. At this point, I decided to make the best of a new experience and enter into the flow of the concert. Was I disappointed? Somewhat. I may have set my sights too high, but it was okay. Joan and I were there for Mary.

The crowd sang along on most of the songs they knew. "I'm not knocking on Heaven's door" and then "Victim of Crime" was played, its eerie strains crushing my earlobes. I had a strange feeling; perhaps this was the one intended for Mary and Greg, but unannounced. A young woman in the next row danced most of the evening. She reminded me so much of Mary, her long, dark hair swaying as she moved, arms waving above her, and wearing a look of unbelievable joy and happiness.

When the concert was over, I said goodbye to my new friend. He said he was sorry that our song was not acknowledged. As we left, we inched our way through the crowd, back over the bridge to reach our car. On the way, we bumped into Dan and his friends outside the parking lot. He seemed somewhat saddened, but his kiss and hug were message enough. It was the right place for all of us to have been that night.

A few years later, I told this story to a young woman who worked at the Albany Rape Crisis Center. She looked at me and said, "I was at a Grateful Dead concert, down in Maryland. I think I heard them say that night that one of their songs was dedicated to someone. I didn't pay much attention to the names. Do you think that that could have been the one meant for Mary?"

I smiled and said, "I don't know." But it was nice to think that perhaps the Grateful Dead had remembered their family members after all.

28

ANNIVERSARIES

The anniversary of Mary's murder, August 16th, always presents a special challenge. In the weeks before, the days before, it's on my mind and it's on the minds of her sisters and brothers. I begin to recall that it was a Friday that the police came, and then the terrible memory of hearing that Mary was dead flashes before me.

In the first year, survivors of homicide victims often play mind games. They pretend that their loved one is away for a while, soon to return. Memories from the year before when they were alive, remain fresh.

After Mary was murdered, I wanted to blot out the whole month of August from the calendar. As the following July rolled around, I could feel the tension begin. I didn't want to think about that next month. Couldn't we jump from July to September?

The summer after Mary's murder I was at the Senator's country home in the Adirondacks for our annual staff weekend. At night, we all bedded down in the many rooms in the large farmhouse. Walking into my room, I saw a colorful poster hung on the wall next to my bed. I felt an empty, sickening feeling overtake me as I read its message: *Essex County Fair, August 16th*. The pain, the sadness, the anger of last year suddenly flashed before me. I was reliving the terrible events of that date.

The passage of time does help. I can now look at the month of August on a calendar without passing over it quickly to go on to September, October, or November. Yet, that actual date, August 16, still remains difficult.

On Mary's third anniversary, I recorded some of my feelings:

> *Last night was even more difficult than today. The anticipation of what today would be took over my emotions. I tried to act as normal as possible: did a load of wash, fixed some dinner. But I could feel myself breaking down, crying, feeling rotten. I began to search for Mary in family photos— what did she look like that last year? I came upon Gerry and Margie's wedding album and stared at her happy face. They are not my favorite pictures of her, but they are a reminder of how happy she was at that time.*
>
> *I telephoned Christine, sorry that I had done so when I could hardly speak. She thought there was something wrong but I explained it was only the date that had me so distressed. We talked for a while and Christine expressed her sadness because Mary would never know (at least not in the way we are used to) her baby, soon to be born. We all grieve in our own ways.*
>
> *The day itself passed quite peacefully. I took a vacation day, and Joan and I planned to spend some time together. We bought some roses and went to the cemetery. A cloudy and cool day turned into a beautiful sunny and warm day. Amanda and Michael were with us. And they took turns putting the roses, one by one, in the green metal holder before Mary's headstone. They were such beautiful red roses. So like Mary, our rose.*

Lighter moments help us along our journey and can be a pathway to healing. On Mary's 16th anniversary, several of us gathered at the cemetery as we had often done. Sitting on the grass, next to her grave, we went around the circle, each recounting a favorite story about Mary.

At Joan's turn, she said, "You know, the words to 'Forever

Young' really ring true. I can't ever picture Mary older than twenty-two."

The rest of us chimed in, shocked to think that she would now be 38 years old, probably married with some children. Then Mike, Joan's husband, spoke up. Very emphatically, he said, "No, I don't think Mary would have any kids."

Shocked by his bluntness, and somewhat defensively, I said, "How can you say that? She loved children. Remember how she was so great with Amanda."

Then he said, smiling widely, "Well, I don't know anyone who makes tie-dye diapers!"

Oh, it felt so good to laugh!

> *Smiles and laughter are another force of healing we can use to fill the hollowness. They propagate spontaneously. The more we smile, the more others smile at us. The more we laugh, the more others laugh with us. The more laughter we hear, the more we want to laugh. Grief tends to scare laughter and smiles away for a time. One, we are profoundly sad. And two, many people withhold their smiles and laughter because they are afraid of being perceived as inappropriate, inconsiderate, or disrespectful with their humor and happiness. No matter how devastating our loss, we eventually need to let ourselves laugh and smile again, even if just a little, and give others permission to do the same around us.*
>
> *Aftermath – In the Wake of Murder, Carrie M. Freitag, p. 185.*

Messages and remembrances from others can raise our spirits. *They must never be forgotten.* POMC National and our Chapter send out yearly anniversary cards. They understand the hunger we experience to know that our loved one is indeed remembered. Several of my friends often commemorate Mary's anniversary – my friend, Rita; my cousin, Helen; and Linda Campion, mother of Kathleen, a beautiful young woman, also cut down in her prime by a drunken driver. On a card, Linda wrote,

Just to let you know I'm thinking of you. The passing years don't change what's happened, but you have so many people walking beside you as you walk so tirelessly to make this world a better place.

Sometimes, we hear from Mary's friends who still remember her. On her tenth anniversary, I was surprised to receive a Mass card from Bob Dowd. I was very moved that he remembered her in this manner. I wrote him a thank you, filling him in on what we as a family had done over the years to keep Mary alive in our hearts.

The next year, I was with Gerry and his family on Mary's anniversary. I recall Gerry met me at the AMTRAK station in Baltimore with a big bouquet of roses. Returning home, a letter from Bob awaited me.

He said he had been overwhelmed by my letter telling him all about our family. He wondered why he had been so "moved on a regular basis by the passing of Mary Regina (both in the sense of her passing from this world and also having passed through my life). Our Blessed Mother has a lot to do with it." The day before Mary's anniversary, August 15th, is the Feast of the Assumption of Mary, the Mother of Jesus, into Heaven.

Bob enclosed a touching essay he wrote entitled, "Remembering Mary Gioia," which is excerpted below:

> *...I saw Mary Gioia many times. More than I can recall. I didn't know her well. Hardly at all, really. I knew who she was. She may not have even known my name. But she did know me.*
>
> *Some of us who lived in the Capital District of New York during the 1980s were part of a group of people often referred to as Dead Heads. We attended as many of the band's concerts as we could, primarily because we liked the music. Also because the people we knew (who also liked the music) were at least a little bit like us. Like Yankee fans, but more so....*
>
> *If I was asked to guess where I first saw Mary Gioia, I would say Sears in Colonie Center....I seem to remember Mary in line at Ticketron, upstairs*

in Sears, near customer service, where we would con-
gregate on mornings that tickets were to go on sale.
I'd swear she wore a pair of green sneakers. I've never
owned green sneakers myself, so the vision sticks
with me.

What I remember most about her was her
smile. I last saw her in California. At Ventura. On the
fairgrounds. By the ocean. She was happy   So was
I....

Mary died very near the Feast of the
Assumption of Our Blessed Mother. That may be one
of the reasons I remember her so well. On August
15th I at least say a prayer for her. Once I had a mass
said for her at a monastery in New York. Sometimes
I light a candle. Her light still shines....Instead of
being sad every August, I guess I should be happy, at
least in part, because I knew Mary Gioia. I am only
sad that I didn't know her any better.

I received another Mass card from Bob on Mary's 15th
anniversary. *Fifteen years pass, like fifteen minutes. Still, we*
remember her. When I realized he was now back in New York, I
sent him an invitation to attend a "Day of Remembrance for
Homicide Victims" held at the Central Park Rose Garden in
Schenectady in September of 2000. He stopped by on his way
home to Amsterdam. There, he met Joan, Christine and Patrick.
It was like a family reunion.

On Mary's 20th anniversary, we commemorated it as we
have so many others. The family members living nearby gathered
together and visited her grave at Park View. We brought her
favorite red roses and huddled under the tree that shades her
grave to share remembrances. As we stood under umbrellas,
Patrick played and sang "Ripple." The last line still rings so true,
If I knew the way, I would take you home.

The rest of the family checked in with me during the day.
It's a time we all must connect.

29

KEEPING HER MEMORY ALIVE

After Mary's untimely death, we were determined that she would continue to play an important role in our family's lives. At first we didn't know how, but soon many paths to that end were before us.

Beginning in 1987, POMC National began a Memorial Wall dedicated to homicide victims. It is now called the "MURDER WALL...Honoring Their Memories." The Wall is made up of many wood panels, each bearing 120 brass plaques with the names, dates of birth and dates of death of murder victims. It travels around the country, especially during Crime Victims' Rights Week, as a reminder that that these were real human beings whose lives were cut short by murder. Our Mary Regina is listed on Wall One.

The next year I contacted the family excitedly, saying, "I just read about a neat idea that one family does to honor their loved one. At Christmas, they pool their money and donate it to a charity in the person's name. Sound good? We could do a combined birthday/ Christmas gift since Mary's birthday is so close to Christmas." With everyone overwhelmingly in favor, we began with Joan, the oldest, and each year we proceed down the line of Mary's siblings who choose a cause and collect donations.

That first year, Joan suggested the Catholic Charities Farano Center for Children in Albany which provided residential care and services for children with pediatric AIDS. On a cold winter day, Joan and I drove over to the Center, located in a private home near Madison Avenue and St. Rose College. A sister, in lay clothing, greeted us at the door.

Joan explained, "I called and spoke to someone and said we were coming over to present a gift from our family in memory of my sister, Mary Gioia."

We were invited inside and Joan briefly explained that our family wanted to honor Mary by helping the children at the Center. When Joan told how Mary died, the sister was close to tears.

About ten children, of differing ages and skills, sat at the tables, eating lunch. A volunteer fed the babies at another table. The children appeared happy and playful, which helped lift our spirits, realizing the terrible disease their little bodies harbored. On the way home, Joan said, "Mom, it broke my heart to see these little children and know what their life will be like."

"I know, I guess we can consider ourselves fortunate no one in our family has a serious health problem like that."

Fast forward a few years later; AIDS quilts were exhibited at the State Museum. I volunteered to assist persons attending who might have grief issues. Standing there, one quilt caught my eye: the Farano Center's. Photos of smiling children, who succumbed to AIDS, were tacked to the quilt. I wondered if we met some of them the day Joan and I brought over Mary's gift.

Chris was the next to choose. That year, 1989, a family priority was to set up a scholarship fund at Schenectady County Community College (SCCC) in Mary's name. We decided on SCCC because she had such a positive experience there. The Arts Council at the time had $1500 in the memorial fund and suggested that Joan and I meet with Dr. Peter Burnham, then President of the college, and Vladia Boniewski, Public Relations Director, to discuss how to proceed. At our meeting, Dr. Burnham told us about three ways we could set up a scholarship.

"The money you've collected thus far can be placed in the general foundation funds or you could award several scholarships in Mary's name until all the funds are gone. Thirdly, and something I think you might want to consider, is a yearly scholarship with the funds endowed each year." He told us we would need at least $5,000 for the last suggestion.

We told him we would speak to the rest of the family and

get back to them with our decision. Of course, everyone agreed we wanted a yearly scholarship. Now we had our work—and campaign—ahead of us.

Vladia arranged an interview for me with a <u>Gazette</u> reporter to start the publicity. Betsy Sandberg wrote a very compassionate article about Mary and what had happened to her. It mentioned we were trying to set up a yearly scholarship. Vladia arranged for a photo of Dr. Burnham, James Gilliland of the Schenectady Arts Council, and me presenting the check to the College. It was published in a later issue of the paper to keep up the momentum for the scholarship.

After a few months of fund raising but still below our goal, I approached the family with another idea. "I'm sending out an appeal letter to everyone on my Christmas card list—and beyond. I think people will respond if they know what we're trying to do."

I was right. After the letters went out, many heeded our plea, with several promising to contribute yearly. Senator Leichter became a very generous contributor to Mary's fund.

I also wrote to several places where Mary had worked. The Bruegger's Bagel Bakery at Stuyvesant Plaza sent a contribution even though the ownership had changed. The Charles Freihofer Baking Company was very generous, writing "Knowing that she was once a part of our 'family' as well, brings this loss so much closer to home."

As the donations continued to trickle in, Lawr telephoned me. At the time, he worked for Salomon Brothers in New York City.

"Mom, Salomon has a matching funds program that can be used if donations are for an educational institution. If we funnel all the money in Mary's scholarship pot through me, we'll be able to double it."

And we did. We pooled the money we had collected, including that year's family birthday and Christmas gift, through Lawr. When Salomon matched the funds, we had enough for the scholarship fund.

Dr. Burnham wrote me a note:

I applaud your persistence and the love and

> commitment you have shown toward your daughter
> Mary's memory. This is one of the most successful
> scholarship efforts in the Foundation's history, and
> you should feel very proud.

Indeed, I was proud of the family's efforts, and, of course, was thrilled as we awarded the first scholarship in May 1990. However, it was a bittersweet moment for me when I walked onto the College Campus and saw so many young people, walking to class and laughing, stark reminders of Mary just a few years before.

After the first scholarship was awarded, I wrote to all our contributors:

> It was with true joy and peace in my heart
> when I presented a $250 check to a very deserving
> young woman. I was sure Mary was looking down
> and smiling. Maria Leonard was the scholarship
> recipient. Ambitious and bright (Phi Beta Kappa),
> Maria also works at a fulltime job to support her
> education...I found out she is from an Italian back-
> ground and was known as "Marriucch" to her fam-
> ily. Excuse the misspelling—my Irish background
> doesn't help me. For those of you like me, Marriuch
> means, "little Mary." Is this a coincidence or is
> something (or someone) else at work here?

And in the third year the scholarship went to another Maria, who lived on Mary Street, and whose mother's name was Mary. Similarities such as these may bring smiles, but I prefer to think of them as signs from Mary. The scholarship awards are larger now as our endowment has grown over the years. As I write, we have presented 17 women with scholarship awards in Mary Regina's name.

Our birthday/Christmas gift plan continued and since its beginnings, we have come up with some varied choices. At his turn, Gerry suggested we use our money to help publish a book for siblings who had a family member with a brain disorder. Mary Ann (Lawr's wife) had contracted Lyme disease, so they chose the Lyme

Borreliosis Foundation, started by a woman who had lost a son to the illness. Robert selected the Heart Association, and Patrick, the AIDS Association. The Make-A-Wish Foundation was Chris' choice, followed by Gerry's selection of the Candlelighter's Association (for children with cancer).

Several closer-to-home agencies also benefited. Our POMC chapter, the Vito A. Masi Memorial Center for Nonviolence, and the Schenectady YWCA Domestic Violence Center have received donations in Mary's name.

In 1994, Dan suggested going forward on Rob's idea of donating to the tree and plaque fund in California. Planting trees and placing a plaque at the Berkeley marina had been in the planning stage for some time. I visited the Berkeley marina in 1992 when I was out in California for the automatic appeal of our case before the California Supreme Court. While there, Jean Stirpe drove me over to the marina. My reaction surprised me. It had been almost seven years since that terrible night but my whole body shook as I stood looking at the rocky shore where Mary was found.

Yoko Ono, speaking about the place where John Lennon was shot, said, "In a way, John's spirit flew away from this building…and so it's a very important place." Ono's words captured our feelings exactly about the spot where Mary and Greg lost their lives and their spirits had flown away.

One day, Jean wrote to me after she had been at the marina with her sailing club. She said when she was there, she thought about Mary and our family. "The contour of the land is slowly changing into a park. Many spend their weekends strolling, walking their dogs and flying kites close by. Each time I'm here I think there should be rose bushes, or trees, planted here to honor Mary. Let's think of a way to do it." The park had now been renamed Cesar E. Chavez Park. How ironic! When I thought of the many times our family refused to buy lettuce if not picked by Chavez' union, I smiled. Could Mary be smiling too?

The idea of a living memorial at the site continued to prick my mind. But how to do it? The opportunity came when a fellow Senate staff member with California connections, put me in touch with an Oakland area assemblyman. His office arranged for me to meet with the park manager of the North Waterfront Park. In October 1993, my friend, Bob Peck, and I, on a trip out west stopped in Berkeley to meet with him. Beforehand, we had lunch at a restaurant at the marina, well known for its seafood and spectacular views of the Bay. As we were seated at our table, I immediately headed for the restroom. My emotions had grabbed me. It took several minutes to steady my nerves and gain control. Our friendly young waitress, long hair pulled back into a bun, was a flashback to Mary. She should be working in a place like this.

After lunch, I met with the manager at the site where Mary and Greg were pulled from the water. I began, "You're aware of what we're trying to do. The Kniffin family and mine are anxious to have a living memorial here for our kids. We've discussed planting some trees and placing a dedication plaque next to them. Will that be possible?"

A kindly man and one who knew the makeup of the land, he answered, "We probably can do that, although the area you're looking at is not exactly suited for planting a tree. We would have to plant further down toward where the sprinkler system begins and the grass starts. Okay, what kind of trees are you thinking about?"

"I've seen some in San Francisco that I really like. I don't know the name of them but they are planted all over the city."

He thought for a moment and then said, "You're probably referring to Eucalyptus ficifolia. But they're more of a southern tree and may not do well over here. Weeping willows, of course, are fast-growing and may be better suited to this area."

I told him we weren't happy about having weeping willows but if that's what would survive there, we'd go along with it.

In May 1995 two trees were planted near some picnic benches. And, yes, they were weeping willows, but all things considered, the name was probably right for the spot. When fully grown, they would provide a place of respite for people using the park. The manager also arranged for a square of concrete to be laid into the ground, awaiting the arrival of our plaque, saying that would prevent it from being stolen. When the plaque was completed, I mailed it to California. It reads:

IN LOVING MEMORY OF
MARY REGINA GIOIA
12/20/62 – 8/16/85
GREGORY ALLEN KNIFFIN
12/19/66 – 8/16/85

Visits to see the trees and the plaque provided us with some family stories, some serious, some amusing. In September 1995, I visited the marina again and took photos of the trees and the plaque. The trees were rather scrawny but since they were within the sprinkler system, I thought they should grow quickly and provide shade for picnickers. The plaque appeared to be well imbedded in the ground

Most of Mary's brothers have been to the site. Robert, on a business trip to San Francisco in February 1999, videotaped his visit to the marina. When he finally found the plaque, with his voice cracking, he said, "I found it. Had to do a little clean-up work here." Rob removed the grass that grew over it.

Robert had not attended the trial so it was quite emotional for him to be at the spot where his sister was murdered. Continuing, he said, "No trees. Nice water fountain there. Couple of picnic tables and picnic benches." This meant that by 1999, the trees were gone. They had not survived the salty breezes blowing in off the Bay.

The next year, Lawr, on a business trip to San Francisco, went to visit the plaque. I received a call from him about 11pm. In an excited voice, he said, "Mom, I'm in Berkeley at the marina. I'm looking for the plaque. Where is it exactly?"

Sleepily, I tried to describe just where the plaque was located. Lawr went off to look. When he called back, although sad he had not located it, he chuckled. Dressed in a business suit, with a taxi waiting for him, he was down on his hands and knees, pushing back grass, looking for the plaque. Several runners passed by and looked at him rather suspiciously. As it was getting dark, he finally had to give up his search.

In August 2002, Joan and I went out to see the plaque with David Kniffin and Dorothy. We were all in Oakland for an evidentiary hearing on our case. David had never seen the plaque and was anxious to do so. He drove us over to Berkeley from the courthouse. It was unusually cool and windy for mid-August. Hopping out of the car, I thought I could lead them directly to where the plaque was. I had been there before. Now even I couldn't locate it. After searching for about 15 minutes, pushing aside high grass from where I thought it should be, we gave up. Maybe Lawrence was right. It really wasn't there anymore.

The next day at court, I spoke to Detective Fred Eihl,

from the Berkeley Police Department, and he volunteered to go over to see if he could find it. He too had no luck but when he called, he gave me a contact number for the Parks, Recreation and Waterfront Department in Berkeley.

Dan was there the day after Mary's nineteenth anniversary, August 17, 2004. He had been there before and seen it, but now even he couldn't find the plaque. After that, I finally contacted the Waterfront Manager of the park, who suggested that I mail him some photos that would clearly show the surrounding landscape and buildings over in Berkeley across the Bay. It worked and he called me to say they found it and had cut down the high grass that had buried it. Our memorial was once again!

Lawr finally saw the plaque on another trip out there in 2005. As he stood looking at it, a woman walked past and asked him about it. After he briefly told her the story of the plaque and the reason for it, she said, "I walk here almost every day. I'll be happy to see that it is kept cleared off. And I'm so sorry for you and your family." Many thanks to that Good Samaritan.

In 2002, it was Dan's turn once again to choose a charity for the family donations. He called and with a chuckle, said, "Mom, we're about to have Mary's name all over the world in bricks!" How true, since he and Kelly suggested that year's gift be sent to Shelter Our Sisters, Pathway to Self Sufficiency, in Bergen County, New Jersey. We purchased a brick in Mary's name to be put in a lovely garden and pathway at Van Saun Park. The pathway *honors the journey that survivors of domestic violence make on their way to wholeness and remembers those unable to make this journey because they did not survive.* We considered Mary was in the latter category.

We have a brick in Mary's name at a Memorial Walkway and Garden at the Journey Home in Rochester. This was Robert's suggestion in 2000. *Journey Home is a comfort care home, whose goal is to provide guidance and support to individuals as they journey through the dying process.* Cycling by one day, Robert stopped to talk to some of the caregivers and learned about the walkway. Now Mary's gift is helping some folks to also *journey home.*

And Patrick suggested that we purchase a brick in Mary's name at the Albany Hudson River Way, a new walkway leading from downtown Albany over to the park next to the Hudson River.

Our brick there reads: *Mary Regina Gioia, 12-20-62 – 08-16-85, Our Beautiful Rose, The Gioia Family.*

Although not part of the Birthday/Christmas gifts, Mary's name is also listed on the very first row of another important brick walkway. The New York State Crime Victims' Memorial is located in a lovely park area directly behind the Legislative Office Building in the City of Albany. When I worked for Senator Leichter, I could see it from our office window. A brick walkway leading up to the Memorial now has over 600 bricks, each bearing the name of a New York State crime victim. This statewide Memorial is very close to my heart as I was involved in its original planning in 1996 as a member of the Capital District Coalition for Crime Victims' Rights. Since then, I have become acquainted with many of the families who also have bricks in the walkway. They, like us, want their loved one to be remembered always.

30

THE COURT CASE – A FOLLOW-UP

Immediately after International was convicted of capital murder and sentenced to death on September 25, 1986, our case transferred to the Office of the Attorney General. District Attorney Jim Anderson had done his job and was no longer involved. When our case advanced to the Attorney General's Office, I received a booklet from the Office of Victims' Services entitled, <u>A Victim's Guide to the Capital Case Process,</u> describing in detail the many phases of a capital case before final execution of a death row inmate. At first glance, it seemed fairly straightforward as a chart outlined the various courts where appeals are allowed. What's missing is a timetable for these appeals, because none exists. Families of homicide victims murdered by a death row inmate in California remain at the mercy of these courts *ad infinitum* - clearly a second victimization. To prove my point, I attach a <u>Timeline of Ralph International Thomas' Appeals</u> in the Appendix.

A lengthy, but thankfully pleasant, association with the Attorney General's Office then began. Any questions or concerns I have, and there have been many, are always answered clearly - and with grace.

My initial contact was in 1989 when I spoke to Gerald Engler (Jerry), assigned to the Ralph International Thomas case. I felt comfortable with Jerry immediately. He gave me his explanation of the automatic direct appeal to the State Supreme Court. "What happened and who did what to whom" was the issue for the seven Justices in examining the trial records to assure International was convicted by correct principles of law. This Court would decide also if there was sufficient evidence presented to convict him of one count of first degree murder. Jerry sent me copies of the briefs submitted by his office and International's lawyers. It was difficult reading—a rehash of the trials—but necessary to keep informed. Since that time, the Attorney General's Office has sent me copies of all actions brought by International's attorneys and their response.

Following what seemed like years of telephone conversations, I finally met Jerry on March 3, 1992, the date the California State Supreme Court conducted a 90-minute hearing on International's direct appeal. I flew out to California and traveled up to Sacramento for the hearing. Jerry argued our case and did it well. The next month he called to say that the Court upheld International's convictions and death sentence.

The next year on a trip to California I arranged to meet Jerry in his San Francisco office. International's lawyers had filed a federal habeas corpus petition. Jerry explained its implications and when he told me there would be no time limit for this appeal to be heard, I knew our road to justice for Mary and Greg would be a long and winding one. While sitting in Jerry's office, I spied boxes and boxes of death penalty cases stacked on the floor, each one marked with the name of an inmate. I shuddered when I caught sight of two or three marked, "Thomas."

Senior Assistant Attorney General Dane Gillette took over the case in 1997 when Jerry moved to another division in the office. I quickly contacted Dane and found that he, too, was extremely sympathetic to our loss and answered all my questions. When Jerry returned to the Criminal Division a few years later, both Dane and he now shared responsibility for our case.

In August 2002, Joan and I went back to Oakland for an evidentiary hearing held at the Alameda County Superior Court, the same court where the original trials were held 16 years before! I met Dane for the first time and Jerry once again, as they both represented the Attorney General's Office at the hearing. Judge Phillip V. Sarkisian was the sitting Judge. International's lawyers brought in witnesses attempting to prove that he was innocent and that someone named "Bo" was responsible for Mary and Greg's deaths. Joan was there for the first few days of the hearing as she presented testimony from her journal to clarify when Mary went out to

California, a point of contention raised by International's lawyers.

The hearing seemed like a family reunion. Jim Anderson actively participated in cross-examining many of the witnesses, with Dane and Jerry ably assisting. David Kniffin and some of his family attended; it was our first meeting in many years. Stephanie Lynch, our Victim Advocate in the original trials, and still working in the Alameda County District Attorney's Office, sat with me for part of the hearing. And I had a long conversation with Fred Eihl, one of the original Berkeley police investigators, after he testified. Only Mary and Greg were missing.

After the hearing, both sides submitted their findings of fact – a summary of the testimony heard at the hearing – to the California Supreme Court. Judge Sarkisian also submitted his report and findings of fact, which Dane felt was quite favorable for us and fully supported the position that Thomas received a fair trial and effective assistance of counsel. Oral arguments from both sides were held before the Supreme Court on December 6, 2005. Finally, a decision of six to one, denying Thomas' petition for a writ of habeas corpus claiming that his defense counsel had failed to adequately investigate evidence that someone other than Thomas committed both murders, was handed down by the Court on March 6, 2006. Over twenty and a half years had passed since Mary and Greg's lives were brutally ended by Ralph Thomas.

It's been a long, long journey, but I have always felt that Mary and Greg and our families have been represented well by Jim Anderson, Jerry Engler and Dane Gillette. Along the way, I have met people I never would have met if these dreadful circumstances had not happened. Most are dedicated individuals doing their best to achieve justice and bring some closure to our case. Perhaps some day it will finally be over.

TIMELINE OF RALPH INTERNATIONAL THOMAS' APPEALS

What follows is a description of the most significant events that have occurred in over 21 years since Ralph International Thomas was convicted of the murders of Mary Gioia and Greg Kniffin and sentenced to death. The reader will notice that there are frequently large gaps in the timeline, sometimes covering a matter of years. The courts that consider death penalty appeals have little or no rules or guidelines regarding how long they may take to decide the appeals. Thus, each appeal can languish for years without any apparent action being taken by the court. Sometimes, the court may be working behind the scenes on these cases, which usually have very long transcripts and records that extend into the thousands of pages. Whatever the reason for the delays, death penalty appeals are generally interminable.

1. September 25, 1986   Thomas' <u>direct appeal</u> is automatically filed with the California Supreme Court pursuant to state law on the same day he is sentenced to death.[1]

---

[1] There are two basic types of appellate review a death-row prisoner can receive. 1) The first type of review is known as a <u>direct appeal</u>, which is limited to an examination of the testimony and exhibits used against the defendant at trial. The defendant gets only one direct appeal to the California Supreme Court. The defendant can then ask the United States Supreme Court to review that direct appeal in what is known in the legal profession as a petition for writ of certiorari; while defendants routinely make such a request, the United States Supreme Court rarely grants certiorari. 2) The second type of review is known as a <u>petition for writ of habeas corpus</u>, which is also sometimes called an indirect appeal or collateral review. A habeas corpus petition is not limited to the trial record, but may go outside that record to introduce new evidence in an effort to show that the defendant's trial was unfair or his attorney was incompetent. In some cases, the defendant may use habeas corpus to introduce new evidence to try to show that he was innocent. A defendant on death row may file many habeas corpus petitions, and may amend or add to his petitions over time. Habeas corpus petitions may be filed in either the state or federal courts, and the defendant may have different attorneys appointed to represent him in the state and federal proceedings. In general, the defendant must raise all of his issues in the state supreme court before the federal court will decide his federal habeas corpus petition.

2. September 12, 1988	Thomas' attorneys file their 207 page legal brief on direct appeal in the California Supreme Court.
3. November 30, 1988	The California Attorney General files a 70 page responsive brief. (It is typical for the Attorney General's legal briefs to be much shorter than the defendant's.)
4. January 16, 1990	Thomas' attorneys file his <u>first habeas corpus petition</u> in the California Supreme Court.
5. April 6, 1990	The Attorney General files an opposition to the first habeas corpus petition.
6. September 4, 1991	The California Supreme Court denies the first habeas corpus petition.
7. October 2, 1991	Thomas files his <u>second habeas corpus petition</u> in the California Supreme Court.
8. October 23, 1991	The California Supreme Court denies the second habeas corpus petition.
9. March 3, 1992	The California Supreme Court conducts a 90-minute hearing on the direct appeal in its courtroom in Sacramento, California.
10. April 23, 1992	The California Supreme Court hands down its written decision upholding Thomas' convictions and death sentence. All seven justices vote to uphold the sec-

ond-degree murder conviction against Mary Gioia. The justices vote 5-2 to uphold the first-degree murder conviction against Greg Kniffin. Since the death sentence requires at least one first degree murder conviction, the two dissenting justices also vote to reverse the death sentence. The two dissenting justices believe that there was not enough evidence to show that Greg Kniffin's murder was premeditated, as is required for first degree murder. However, the five justices in the majority, in an opinion authored by Justice Panelli, state, "We are satisfied that the evidence reasonably justified the jury's conclusion that defendant formed and acted on a deliberate plan to kill." In particular, the majority emphasizes that Thomas' rifle required manual removal of the expended shell and reloading of a fresh shell before it could be fired a second time and that the jury could have reasonably concluded that Thomas had a motive to murder Greg in order to eliminate him as a witness to the murder of Mary.[2]

11. October 6, 1992

Thomas' attorneys file a petition for writ of certiorari with the United States Supreme Court asking that court to review the direct appeal decision of the California Supreme Court.

[2] Believe it or not, Thomas' direct appeal, which took three and one-half years to decide, is resolved much more quickly than the typical direct appeal in a California death penalty case, which can often take more than 10 years to decide.

| 12. January 11, 1993 | The United States Supreme Court denies Thomas' request to review the direct appeal decision of the California Supreme Court. |

13. February 19, 1993   Thomas asks the United States District Court to appoint an attorney for him to handle his federal habeas corpus petition and to stay all execution proceedings until his federal case is concluded. United States District Judge Marilyn Hall Patel grants his request for a stay of any attempt to set an execution date.

14. September 2, 1993   Judge Patel appoints an attorney to represent Thomas in his federal habeas corpus case.

15. April 15, 1996   Thomas' attorneys file a petition for writ of habeas corpus in Judge Patel's court (his third habeas corpus petition overall).

16. May 24, 1996   The California Attorney General files a motion in Judge Patel's court asking that she order Thomas to go back to the California Supreme Court to present the issues that he has never raised in that court before.

17. August 14, 1996   Judge Patel issues an order permitting Thomas' attorneys to take depositions of certain Rainbow Village denizens and Deadheads and of a number of the trial participants, including James Chaffee and Jim Anderson,

in an effort to determine whether Chaffee performed incompetently by failing to investigate whether a Deadhead named "Bo" had anything to do with the murders.

18. November 14, 1996

Thomas' trial attorney James Chaffee is deposed about his trial representation. During the course of that deposition, Chaffee gives the following testimony regarding what Thomas told him about the crimes: "There are only two things that ever led me to waiver in the—the thought that he might have done this. One was, I was always concerned throughout that—that the rifle would be found, and I said to him one time, 'I hope they don't find that thing,' you know, and he . . . looked at me and said, 'Don't worry about it. They're not gonna find it.' And from the way he said it and his body attitude, it indicated to me that perhaps he knew what had happened to that rifle. . . . His response to me in that situation led me to believe that he had some notion of what had actually become of the rifle, which was why he could be so certain that the police wouldn't find it. The other thing . . . was similar. It had to do with the clothes he was wearing that night . . . . He had made an excursion to a laundromat and washed some clothes that night, and people had testified earlier, I think, that he had been wearing a particular set of clothes that the police never found, that were never located. . . . And I asked him if . . . he knew what had become of those clothes, whether or not he had laundered them. I believe my—my belief is that he indicated that he had laundered those clothes and put them—and I know for a fact he indicated to me that he disposed of those clothes by putting them in a poor box in Berkeley, which is a collection box for, you know, clothing to be given to the poor, the needy. So those two things—his certainty that the rifle would not be found and the fact that he had laundered and then gotten rid of the clothes that he'd apparently been wearing the night of the murders—led me to believe that these were factual circumstances that might indicate he had something to do with these murders." Because Thomas had a right not to incriminate himself and his conversations with his lawyer were private, no one but Chaffee knew about these statements until the deposition. However, once Thomas asked to have his convictions set aside because of Chaffee's alleged poor representation, he waived the shield of the attorney-client privilege and his statements could be exposed.

19. May 7, 1997		Judge Patel orders petitioner to go back to the California Supreme Court to present the issues that he has not previously raised with that court, including the allegation that "Bo" may be the real killer.
20. August 1, 1997		Thomas' attorneys file his third habeas corpus petition in the California Supreme Court (his <u>fourth habeas corpus petition</u> overall), presenting the issues outlined in Judge Patel's May 1997 order.
21. October 24, 1997		The California Attorney General files opposition to Thomas' third state (and fourth overall) habeas corpus petition.
22. June 13, 2001		The California Supreme Court issues an order directing that the Alameda County Superior Court take evidence focusing on the question whether trial attorney Chaffee failed to investigate and present evidence that another person (the mysterious "Bo") had killed Mary and Greg.
23. August 12, 2002		A hearing begins before Judge Phillip V. Sarkisian of the Alameda County Superior Court concerning the issues in the California Supreme Court's order. The hearing (called an "evidentiary hearing") will be held on a total of eight days in

August, November, and December 2002. Alameda County Deputy District Attorney Jim Anderson comes back into the case to cross-examine Thomas' witnesses at the evidentiary hearing, assisted by representatives from the California Attorney General's office. Thomas has three attorneys presenting his case. Many witnesses are called to testify about what, if anything, they know about "Bo." Pat Gioia and her daughter Joan attend the first days of the hearing along with David Kniffin and his sister. Joan testifies about some entries in her diary establishing when Mary left for California, discrediting several of the witnesses offered by Thomas's attorneys who testified that Mary was present in Berkeley in the Spring of 1985.

24. April 29, 2003

Judge Sarkisian issues a 57 page report to the California Supreme Court rejecting all of the allegations about trial attorney Chaffee. Specifically, Judge Sarkisian finds that "Chaffee conducted an adequate investigation consistent with his theory of the case and the information available to him" and that Thomas' attorneys failed to prove that "Bo" "was connected in any way to the murders." Judge Sarkisian finds that the witnesses offered by Thomas' attorneys at

241

the evidentiary hearing were not believable, that some of the statements attributed to them were actually provided to them by an investigator for Thomas, that they had no firsthand or personal knowledge about the murders, and thus that they could not have been called to testify at trial.

25. November 11, 2003

Both Thomas' attorneys and the California Attorney General file their written briefs in the California Supreme Court concerning Judge Sarkisian's report. Thomas' brief is 252 pages long and asks the Supreme Court to disregard Judge Sarkisian's report and issue a favorable ruling to Thomas. The Attorney General's brief is 76 pages long and asks the Supreme Court to approve Judge Sarkisian's findings.

26. December 12, 2005

The California Supreme Court holds a hearing on whether to approve Judge Sarkisian's findings.

27. March 6, 2006

The California Supreme Court issues an opinion upholding Judge Sarkisian's findings and ruling that Thomas' efforts to show that a mysterious man named "Bo" might have been the killer do "absolutely nothing to undermine the case actually presented against Thomas."

28. April 12, 2006

The California Supreme Court

issues an order formally denying Thomas' third state habeas corpus petition.

Next Steps

The case will go back to Judge Patel's court for her decision on Thomas' federal habeas corpus petition. We expect that the case will be put back on Judge Patel's docket by the early summer of 2006, but there is no way to predict when she will decide the case. Judge Patel's is not the last word, as Thomas can appeal an adverse decision to the United States Court of Appeals for the Ninth Circuit. A federal habeas corpus case can take many twists and turns and result in multiple appeals to the Ninth Circuit, <u>and there are no deadlines that the federal courts must follow in issuing their rulings</u>. Sadly, based on the experience of the California Attorney General's Office, many years may yet pass before all of Thomas' appeals will come to an end. More than four times as many of California's death row inmates have died due to natural causes or suicide than from the execution of a death sentence since the reinstitution of California's death penalty law in 1977. Unfortunately, the appeals process as it currently exists offers little hope for closure to the surviving families and loved ones of murder victims.

NOTES and AFTERTHOUGHTS

PREFACE
'The rose is the most prominent image: Robert Hunter. Jackson, Blair, *Grateful Dead – the music never stopped*, New York, N.Y.: Delilah Communications Ltd., 1983, pp. 152, 153.

CHAPTER 1, page 16
Their first question took me off guard:
It is extremely important that death notification be performed in a compassionate and professional manner. It is a difficult task to tell another person that a loved one is dead but with the proper training it can be done with the least possible harm to the receiver of the bad news. MADD holds training seminars tailored for law enforcement, clergy, chaplains, coroners, advocates, EMTs and other professionals to teach them how to "break the tragic news with concern for the messenger and compassion for the survivor." I have attended two of these very worthwhile seminars. I am grateful that the two Niskayuna police officers who came to my house to advise me of my daughter's murder acted in a compassionate and professional manner. For most survivors, how they were notified and told of a homicide or tragic death, will remain with them forever. Therefore, it is crucial that it is performed correctly.

CHAPTER 4, page 30
Uppermost in our minds was whether I:
One of the most difficult decisions a family must make is whether to see their loved one's body after the murder. Should your last mental picture be as you remember them in life, or as they were desecrated by a murderer's vicious act? It's a decision one can never fully reconcile. It's taken some time for me to feel comfortable with our decision not to view Mary's body. We relied on others who had been with her to identify her, and the photo identification in her wallet. During the trial, the district attorney displayed photos of the crime scene, including gruesome pictures of Mary's body. He strongly discouraged us from looking at them, even from viewing them in his office privately. I now believe I made the right decision, for when I picture Mary, she is as she was when I last saw her – beautiful and whole.

To assist families who view this dilemma differently, Parents Of Murdered Children has held workshops at some of its annual conferences on "Crime Scene Picture Viewing." Family members who actually viewed photos of their loved one's body after a homicide share their experience. Faith I. Uhler-Myers, Program Manager of the Victim/Witness Program, York County (Pennsylvania) District Attorney's Office, attended one of these workshops in 1999. Since then, her program has offered the service of Crime Scene Photo Viewing to homicide survivors. Myers says it's not openly advertised because not all homicide survivors request it. If it is, they work with the family beforehand to sort out what they might expect to get from the process, including what they want and don't want to see. The family is prepared for the viewing beforehand and a support person is present if requested.

CHAPTER 5

Page 37: The Oakland Tribune printed a short piece: "Body found floating in Berkeley lagoon," *The Tribune,* August 17, 1985.

Page 37: On Sunday, a longer story appeared: Evangelista, Benny, "2nd body found in the bay near Berkeley Marina, *The Tribune,* August 18, 1985.

Page 38: By Monday, the 19th,: Staff and wire reports, "Niskayuna grad slain in Calif. Woman, 22, shot with companion," *Times Union,* August 19, 1985.

Page 38: The Gazette also quoted Garcia,: Wilkin, Jeff, "Murder of Niskayuna Woman Under Investigation in Calif., *Schenectady Gazette*, August 19, 1985.

Page 39: He took the call from The Knickerbocker News.: Smith, Greg B., "Former Niskayuna woman, 22, found shot to death in California," *The Knickerbocker News,* August 19, 1985.

Page 39: The media likes to put their own spin: DelVecchio, Rick, "'Deadheads' Had Been Lovers, Hunt for Clues in Berkeley Killings," *SanFrancisco Chronicle,* August 19, 1985.

Page 41: A local reporter, Joe Mahoney,: Mahoney, Joe, "Police lack suspects in California slaying, Family grieves in Niskayuna," *Times Union,* August 20, 1985.

CHAPTER 6, page 43
We were not aware of the local television station:

Families of crime victims should have more privacy rights. It is sometimes a family's first experience in dealing with story-hungry reporters and photographers. To speak to the media—especially on camera—or to be photographed, should be the personal choice of the victims' family members. "Grief should not be a spectator sport" (Terry Anderson). If it's possible, the family should have a person experienced in dealing with the media with them if they choose to do an interview.

On the other hand, the media can be of assistance to crime victims. In unsolved cases, the media can keep the story alive in a search for the victim or for the murderer. In my own case, Judy Sanders remembered that she had interviewed me shortly after Mary's murder. We met again at an Assembly Press Conference many years later where I spoke on gun violence. She approached me and did a follow-up story on our case, with additional publicity given to the New York State Crime Victims' Memorial in Albany which I wanted highlighted.

Interview with Judy Sanders, WRGB Channel 6, Schenectady, New York, August 19, 1985.

CHAPTER 7, page 49
Bertrand Fay, our long-time priest friend:
Recently, I met with Bertrand Fay who gave the Memorial homily and presided at Mary's burial. Since so many years had passed, I asked him if he remembered what he said at those services.

> *"Yes, it's been a long time but I'll try to recall. When I learned about Mary's death, I thought, my God, this shouldn't happen to them; it shouldn't happen to anyone. When you take this marvelous achievement that I felt your family was, and then that shattering experience occurs, it was a very important moment."*

Mary was murdered on August 16th, the day after the Feast of the Assumption of the Blessed Lady, the mother of Jesus. I asked Bert if he would have tied that into his homily. Again, straining to recall, he said,

> *There were a couple of things operating for me, which I may or may not have referred to. First of all, there was her name, the whole Victoria,*

Regina thing that we fooled around with. No matter what you (and Vito) thought and what you chose, I always thought Victoria [should be her name].

He said that August 16th, the day of Mary's death, was a special time each year for his father. In the old Church calendar, it was the Feast of St. Joachim, the Blessed Virgin's father, and he might have included some words about that in his homily. He ended his reflections on his homily by assuring me that Mary was indeed okay.

The mystery of the Assumption spoke to our ability to transcend to her already having transcended. I can't believe for a single moment that at that time she (our Mary) was in any way alone, unaided, unassisted, that the holy ones were not somehow present. I think when that happens you are already caught up instantly in God, in Christ, in the Great Mother. So the name, the Victoria part, my part, I thought, I know she's all right now. **Our problem is to become okay.**

As Bert spoke, my thoughts were of Mary in her last moments. This remains the most painful image I must deal with. He said,

By that same token, I couldn't believe there wasn't a presence to her at that moment.

CHAPTER 8, page 57
We gathered around the tree:

Bertrand Fay told me of his memory of the day of Mary's burial:

I remember that I came to your house first. And then I remember driving there. It was very, very hot. And we walked up this hill. And it was blinding light and heat. Not a great deal of shade. That's where the plot was. And there was a door-mat size plastic green cover there. And on top of it was the container, the urn.

My feeling was this is not enough to deal with. We needed something big. If I may say so, in our culture, we need to do it like the Hindus. We need the Ganges, the flames, everything you know, the washing of the ashes in the Great River. That's

what you need. But we didn't have that. And I think
we have learned.

> *I've had two or three burial services since*
then and I spoke to that sort of thing, that this is not
enough. And I think that was Robert's challenge
because he sang again. And, I remember the text of
his song was on the neck of his guitar—to help him
with the pressure of the moment. And at the end, he
didn't seem to know what to do, and he took it off
the guitar and put it around the urn.

CHAPTER 11, page 97
Parents Of Murdered Children (POMC):
Parents Of Murdered Children and Other Survivors of Homicide Victims was started in 1978 by Bob and Charlotte Hullinger, whose daughter, Lisa, was murdered in Germany. POMC is a self-help support group offering emotional support and friendship to persons who survive the violent death of a loved one by homicide. POMC, Inc. (the national organization) has its offices in Cincinnati, Ohio. There are chapters in over 25 states. The Albany/Capital District Chapter was started in 1982 by Robin Stambler and has continued to hold monthly meetings since that time.

CHAPTER 13, page 109
I had a yellow pad on which I took copious notes: Freitag, Carrie M., *Aftermath – In the Wake of Murder,* Ellicott City, MD: CHEVRON Publishing Corporation, 2003, p. 11.

CHAPTER 17, page 143
But I found strength from an unlikely source,: Stein, Ruthe, "A Last Vigil for Their Kids – Why parents attend trials of their children's killers," <u>San Francisco Chronicle</u>, May 15, 1986.

CHAPTER 18, page 151
The Judge also said he would rule: Cooper, J.E., "DA rests case in Rainbow Village trial," <u>The Daily Californian</u>, May 21, 1986.

CHAPTER 19 159
Page   : Then Johnson continued and told how he was in Berkeley: Cooper, J.E., "Witness sought in Thomas trial," <u>The</u>

Daily Californian, May 23, 1986.
Page 161: Anderson continued to argue hard,: Cooper, J.E., "Jury deliberates Rainbow Village case," *The Daily Californian,* May 30, 1986.
Page 162: Again, The Daily Californian: Ibid.
Page 162: The Daily Californian article concluded,: Ibid.

CHAPTER 20, page 170
The courtroom scene was described as follows: Cooper, J.E., "Jury convicts Thomas of Rainbow Village murders, *The Daily Californian,* June 6, 1986.

CHAPTER 21, page 173
Defendants have rights in the U.S. Constitution, victims do not:
Over the years, several attempts have been made to pass an amendment to have victims' rights included in the U.S. Constitution similar to the "rights of the accused." None have been successful. A number of states (33 in 2004) have adopted victim rights amendments to their individual State Constitutions. New York State is not in this list. In 2004, after a long battle to once again amend the U.S. Constitution, a Federal Victim Rights Law, H.R. 5107, passed, which was viewed by many victim organizations as a partial victory. The statute establishes powerful enforcement mechanisms and authorizes funding to help implement the law, including free legal clinics for victims. A coalition of victim rights groups, including POMC, worked with Congress to write this legislation.

CHAPTER 23, page 187
He reminded them that she admitted she met with the defense team: Concurring and Dissenting Opinions of California State Supreme Court Justices, filed in Supreme Court on April 23, 1992, The People v. Ralph International Thomas.

CHAPTER 24
Page 191: As I read them, I felt I was out there: Spears, Larry, "Jury urges death for killer of two," *The Tribune,* June 21, 1986.
Page 192: Another newspaper described International's demeanor: Martinez, Don, "Jury wants Rainbow Village killer executed," *The Examiner,* June 21, 1986.

CHAPTER 25
Page 197: Jean sent me an article that reported: Lane, Del, "Rainbow Village killer's lawyers trying to save him from death," *The Tribune*, September 5, 1986.
Page 200: On September 25, 1986, Alameda County Superior Court Judge: Jones, Will, "Man sentenced to die for two 1985 murders," *The Tribune*, September 26, 1986.

CHAPTER 26
Page 205: Now, …I finally wrote Mary's story. Gioia, Patricia M, "Finished Business?," *Victims' Voice,* Victims Of Crime Advocacy League of New York State, Inc. Newsletter, Winter 1988.
Page 205: On Sunday, May 1, 1988, the steps of the New York State Capitol:

National Crime Victims' Rights Week is commemorated in the Capital District each year since that first ceremony held on the Capitol steps. The Capital District Coalition for Crime Victims Rights (CDCCVR) grew out of this effort. POMC and VOCAL were part of the founding groups, along with RID, MADD, the Albany County Crime Victim and Sexual Violence Center, the Michele E. Martin Memorial Foundation and Albany STOP-DWI. CDCCVR has expanded into a much wider and more comprehensive group of individuals and victim organizations that interact with crime victims in the six counties of Albany, Rensselaer, Saratoga, Schenectady, Warren and Washington Counties. In 1996, the Coalition established the New York State Crime Victims' Memorial on the grounds of the Empire State Plaza in Albany. A brick walkway with the names of New York State crime victims leading up to the Memorial was started in 1997. Two walkways now contain over 600 names of crime victims and more are added each year during Crime Victims' Rights Week.

CHAPTER 28, page 219
Oh, it felt so good to laugh!: Freitag, Carrie M., *Aftermath – In the Wake of Murder,* Ellicott City, MD: CHEVRON Publishing Corporation, 2003, p. 185.

MARY REGINA'S FAMILY

Father: VITO MICHAEL GIOIA, Child Psychologist, Chief of Children Services, Syracuse Developmental Center, deceased, 9/14/77.

Mother: PATRICIA M. GIOIA, retired New York State Senate employee, victim advocate.

Siblings:

JOAN FRANCES GIOIA CELENTANO, Emergency Room Nurse; b. 1953; married Michael Celentano in 1980. Two children: Amanda Christine, b. 1983; Michael Vito, b. 1986.

CHRISTINE MARIE GIOIA JOYCE, Health Care Worker; b. 1954; married Jeffrey Joyce in 1982. One child: Sean Patrick, b. 1988.

GERARD ANTHONY GIOIA, Pediatric Neuropsychologist; b. 1956; married Margie Genau in 1985. Three children: Theresa Rose, b. 1988; Maria Christine, b. 1990; Anthony Robert, b. 1993.

LAWRENCE JOSEPH GIOIA,Wall Street Market Data Firm Entrepreneur; b. 1957; married Mary Ann DeFrank in 1982. Two children: Laura Elizabeth, b. 1987; Kathryn Mary, b. 1990.

ROBERT ANDREW GIOIA, Manufacturer Representative; b.1959; married Brenda Gavagan in 1987. Two children: Madeline Joan, b. 1990; Maureen Patricia, b. 1993.

PATRICK DAVID GIOIA, Wine and Spirits Sales Representative; b.1961; married Elizabeth Gist in 1991. Two children: Caroline Jacqueline, b. 1995; Colin Patrick, b. 1999.

DANIEL PAUL GIOIA, Corporate Finance Professional; b. 1966; married Kelly Laccetti in 1996. Three children: Erin Mary, b. 1998; Daniel Vito, b. 2000; Andrew Joseph, b. 2003.

WHAT OTHERS SAY

"Pat Gioia is a dynamic woman who took a horrific personal tragedy to the steps of the Capitol of New York State. Her advocacy on behalf of crime victims has ensured that laws are enacted to implement change in the criminal justice system to give victims a voice. Her mission for the last 20 plus years has been to support Parents of Murdered Children and other survivors of homicide with love and compassion. I admire her and have learned so much from her through the years. Mary Regina's short life is forever celebrated and with Pat's determination it is not forgotten."

-Christina Hernandez, MSW, Commissioner
New York State Crime Victims Board

"Pat Gioia is a unique individual with a sense of humor and motherly doting that belies her sense of purpose and strong determination to achieve whatever she sets out to accomplish. Whatever she asks of you, you cannot deny her request. Her children are very fortunate to have such a wonderfully caring and resilient mom.

"I met Pat several years after the tragedy that struck her family in August 1985. The death of her daughter, Mary Regina, propelled Pat into the media limelight and into a life that was forever changed by her daughter's murder. With a determination worthy of a general going into battle, Pat harnessed the energy of the tragedy that had befallen her family and led the charge for crime victims' rights in New York State. While she could not change what occurred to her and Mary Regina, she was determined to change what would happen to crime victims in the aftermath of the crime. Because of her unyielding single-mindedness, she has forever altered the landscape of crime victims' rights in New York State. Where victims once were barely acknowledged and often barred from participating in the criminal justice process, crime victims now have a voice in the criminal justice system. We all have been enriched by Pat's dedication and compassion. Through Pat, we also have come to know Mary Regina and share in the sadness of her loss."

-Lorraine Felegy, Deputy Counsel
New York State Division of
Criminal Justice Services

"I can honestly say that in my many years in the Criminal Division of the Attorney General's Office, getting to know the two of you (David Kniffin and Pat Gioia) was one of the most rewarding experiences I have had. When constantly working on criminal appeals, we rarely have opportunity to come into contact with the people we are serving. It is sometimes easy to lose sight of the very real human impact our work has on victims and their families. You helped me to keep sight of that fact, and, as a result, helped me to be a better lawyer."

-Gerald A. Engler
Senior Assistant Attorney General
State of California Department of Justice

"Pat Gioia was the first person I met when moving to Schenectady; she was passing election petitions for the McGovern race for President. I asked her if she could introduce a teenage friend for my daughter to meet since she knew no one at her new high school. Pat not only did that right away, but also got me on the Democratic Committee. Pat later served as Treasurer (volunteer) for RID (Remove Intoxicated Drivers). She was also working for Senator Franz Leichter and managing her large family of eight.

"The day her daughter, Mary, was murdered in faraway California, her life plunged into shock and then anger. She added another cause to her many activist duties...helping other parents of murdered children find some relief and empathy.

"Shortly she became the POMC chapter leader, appearing often in the media with letters to the editor, public radio and TV, managing victims' rights and awareness programs. Pat is also my good next-door neighbor, ready with a joke or suggestion (don't forget to vote). Her local newsletter comes out on time, self-written and produced. You can depend on Pat, as so many victims in the New York Capital Area do.

-**Doris Aiken, President of Remove**
Intoxicated Drivers (RID)

"When a fun-loving 'liberal-minded' family is faced with a tragedy of the worst kind, the cruel loss of a loved one – daughter, sister, friend – it changes the way that one thinks, acts, and feels forever. Besides always missing our dear sweet Mary

253

immensely, to consider that another human being would take her precious life has rocked all of our foundations of humanity. As a family, we have all tried to understand and cope with the loss of Mary in each of our own unique ways – all as a result of one man's selfish, disturbed brutality. Who would have ever thought we would have to wrestle so personally with the concepts of 'murder' and 'death penalty.' Such a horrific experience shakes you to the core and makes you question the roots of humankind. And yet the wonderful spirit of our sister, daughter, friend continues to live on in each one of us and in our own children every time a sweet, innocent act of kindness is enacted in our families. And that spirit of Mary is present in the strength, caring and persistence of our determined mother as she has turned this unimaginable tragedy into something positive by helping others cope with their own tragic losses. We have all had to go on without our sweet daughter, sister, friend but Mary lives on in all of us!"

-Gerard A. Gioia, PhD, Director,
Pediatric Neuropsychology
Program, Children's National
Medical Center

ABOUT THE AUTHOR

Patricia (Malone) Gioia has been a Chapter Leader in Parents Of Murdered Children (POMC) since 1988 and editor of the chapter's newsletter for 15 years. With other victim organizations, she helped launch the Capital District Coalition for Crime Victims' Rights, which advocates for crime victims in six counties. Pat has served on the New York State Crime Victims Board Advisory Council and on the Attorney General's Crime Victims Advisory Board. Her essays on Mary Regina's murder have appeared in _Bereavement: A Magazine of Hope and Healing_. She has seven adult children and 15 grandchildren, and resides in Schenectady, New York.